THE COMPLETE
KAYAK FISHERMAN

THE COMPLETE KAYAK FISHERMAN

Ric Burnley

BURFORD BOOKS

Printed in the United States of America.

10   9   8   7   6   5   4   3   2   1

Library of Congress Cataloging-in-Publication Data
      Burnley, Eric B.
      The complete kayak fisherman / Eric Burnley.
            p.   cm.
      Includes index.
      ISBN 978-1-58080-147-8
      1. Fishing.   2. Kayaking.   I. Title.

  SH441.B89   2007
  799.1—dc22   2007028468

CONTENTS

To my dad Eric for taking me fishing,
to my wife Natasha for encouraging me to go fishing,
and to my fishing buddy Kevin for going with me.
Thanks.

Introduction

The cool thing about kayak fishing is that it combines two great pursuits: kayaking and fishing. Taken alone, each of these sports is worthy of fanatical passion. Together, fishing out of a kayak warrants extremist devotion.

Unlike sailboarding, waterskiing, or kite surfing, kayak fishing isn't simply the fusion of two separate sports—it's the complement of two sports. We kayak to catch fish.

In fact, kayak fishing proves that opposites attract. While paddling a kayak is calm, quiet, and relaxing, chasing fish is violent, exciting, and nerve racking. If fishing is mostly a mental exercise, kayaking is a physical one. Paddling a kayak is about as strenuous as taking a brisk walk, and fishing from one can be as simple or as outlandish as you choose.

I came to kayak fishing as a fisherman, not a kayaker. In fact, I had never paddled a kayak before I went fishing from one. But I had spent a lot of time on the water. I grew up with a fishing rod in my hand.

For me, the cool thing about kayak fishing is that it's a means to an end. Already a rabid surf fisherman, I wanted to extend my range beyond the shore break, and I had heard of dudes using kayaks to get

A kayak's light weight and maneuverability allow anglers to use lighter tackle to target bigger fish. Try catching flounder on a ¼-ounce jig and Gulp jig from a boat.

off the beach. After some research I picked up a boat and christened it by terrorizing the backwaters with light tackle. But I soon grew restless and began to set my sights on bigger game. My first target was bull red drum. I knew these fish swam close to shore—in the surf, even—and could be reached with a 'yak. After settling on a promising location, outfitting my craft, and drafting my fishing buddy Kevin Whitley into the plan, we set off for the shoals of Virginia's Eastern Shore. Well, to make a long story a little longer, we caught a couple of nice reds that night and returned to the launch alive—encouraging us to set our sights a little farther and a lot higher. Since then Kevin and I have taken our kayaks places people wouldn't dream of taking their boats and caught fish people wouldn't think possible. And we've had way too much fun along the way.

Which is the cool thing about kayak fishing: It doesn't require you to reinvent the wheel, but it can be the mother of invention. For the most part, fishing out of a kayak is the same as fishing out of any boat, and paddling a fishing kayak is the same as paddling any kayak. That said, an angler will have to take into account the limits that a kayak places on tackle and range, while a paddler will need a few new skills to chase down fish. These pages are a compilation of what I know and what I've learned. Over the hours, and hours, and hours, I've spent on the water in my kayak, I've developed a practical approach to fishing out of a small plastic boat. Where my own experience runs thin, I've called in some of the best kayak anglers in the sport and the most knowledgeable techies in the industry.

For that reason, this book will not cover fishing or kayaking; it will cover kayak fishing. Attempting to bridge the narrow fissure between these two sports, I'll explain how to turn a kayak into a fishing machine and a fisherman into a kayaker. From choosing, outfitting, and rigging a paddle-powered fish destroyer to putting it on the water and on the fish, this book will get a newbie off the ground and teach an old dog some new tricks. One thing this book will not do, however, is profess the "right way" to fish out of a kayak—this is just one way to do it.

And that's the cool thing about kayak fishing: It is what you make it. From diehards to lazy afternoon drifters, anyone can fish from a kayak. These cheap plastic boats require little maintenance; they're convenient to store and transport, simple to rig and repair, and a breeze to launch and recover. Adding a kayak to your fishing arsenal will add hours to your fishing log—it's easy to stop by the local watering hole after work and get in a quick session on the 'yak. Even veteran anglers find a new respect for the species they chase and the water they fish. There is nothing like being dragged around by a sea monster and then wrestling the leviathan into your boat, toe-to-toe, face-to-face, so close you can smell the bait on the fish's breath. Totally prehistoric.

Kayak anglers can go where no boat can go, but that doesn't mean they can't go where boats do go. Nothing beats paddling into a traffic jam of boaters and pulling fish from beneath their propellers.

In fact, kayak fishing is so cool, you will wonder how you ever fished without one. Ultimately you'll use your paddle boat in ways you could never have dreamed when the idea of fishing from one first struck you. The only thing limiting a kayaker's fishing is the kayaker's imagination.

And that's cool.

1

Choosing a Kayak

Picking out a kayak is like picking out a best friend. After all, kayak and kayaker will be together for a long time, through thick and thin, sharing many great memories and working together to get out of some hairy situations. So a prospective kayak should be chosen carefully, not only for its characteristics as a watercraft—speed, maneuverability, and stability—but also for its qualities as a fishing platform: comfort, layout, and storage capacity.

With the recent explosion in popularity of kayak fishing, nearly every major boat manufacturer is adding an "Angler" edition to its line. Whether the company is actually designing a fishing-specific boat or simply throwing a couple of rod holders and a tacklebox onto a current model, the variety of fishing kayaks available to anglers is vast.

In fact, there are so many boats available and so many types of fishing open to kayaking that you can find the perfect boat to match your style of fishing. The boat must satisfy not just your needs as an angler but your needs as a kayaker, too. It must be comfortable to paddle, able to handle the weight of both you and your gear, and capable of going the places you'll take it. In addition, a fishing kayak will need to accommodate you while still offering plenty of room to store tackle, flat spaces on the deck to mount rod holders and gadgets, and large hatches for extra storage.

Even though each fishing kayak seems to satisfy these requirements, one boat may be better suited to one type of fishing or fisherman than another. A boat that will cover miles of choppy open water will be a beast to maneuver through backwater creeks and canals. A boat that can carry a 300-pound paddler and his entire collection of rods, reels, and tackle will bog down a small-framed fly angler. Sight casters who want to stand, trollers who want to pull lures, waders who want to walk, and stealth anglers looking to sneak up on their quarry will each need a different boat. One kayak does not fit all kayak anglers.

Arguments rage at paddle shops and on Web forums about what boat is ideal for which type of fishing, and kayak manufacturers love to tout the latest one-boat-fits-all model. But your final decision will be a personal one. When choosing a new kayak, put all of the advice, all of the fishing kayaks, and all of the intended applications together. Next, pick the top three candidates and give each a thorough test paddle. Then pick out your new best friend.

SOTs Versus SINKs

Kayak fishing evolved out of the two pursuits that make up its name: kayaking and fishing. Some kayaker somewhere took a rod with him when he went for a paddle, or some fisherman somewhere bought a kayak and used it to chase fish where they were once inaccessible. Boom—the big bang—kayak fishing crawled out of the primordial ooze.

Since then the sport has exploded. First, anglers had to modify the kayaks that were available at the time, bastardizing boats that were intended for other uses—cutting, melting, drilling, and gluing until they had transformed their kayaks into fishing machines. Today there are specific boats for specific applications, from flats to open ocean to rivers to ponds. Each angler can find the perfect fit.

Kayaks basically come in two flavors for fishing: sit-on-tops (SOTs) and sit-in kayaks (SINKs). As the name implies, with the latter you sit inside a large hole in the hull. With a sit-on-top model, there is no hole in the hull (besides the hatches); you sit atop the boat the same way you might sit atop a surfboard. Both types are most commonly made of molded hard plastic that is nearly indestructible. Each model has advantages and disadvantages for paddlers, and each model has its place in fishing. No one style will satisfy everyone.

SOTs

By far the most popular kayaks for fishing are sit-on-top models. With a wide-open cockpit that provides plenty of space to mount fishing gear and a broad, stable hull, these boats are ideal for anglers even if they are slower to paddle. SOTs are also more forgiving in rough seas—they won't take on water, and they're easier to remount if you should fall out. Moreover, it is considerably easier to get out of a SOT than a SINK, making this a more user-friendly option, especially for people who aren't in the best physical condition.

The main drawback of sit-on-top kayaks is that they are slow and inefficient. To compensate for the paddler sitting higher off the water, kayak designers must make a sit-on-top kayak wider, its bottom flatter. More boat in the water creates greater drag, making the SOT harder to paddle and maneuver. Another drawback is that the SOT paddler is completely exposed to the elements. Rain, wind, cold, and blazing sun beat you from head to toe. At least with a SINK, you're covered from the waist down. In general, SOTs also have less belowdeck dry storage. If you plan to use your boat for camping, you'll be better served by a SINK in which you can stow tent, sleeping bag, and several days' worth of supplies.

Still, despite the disadvantages, SOTs are the most popular fishing kayaks. Most kayak fishermen who came to the sport from fishing get into a sit-on-top. These boats are very user-friendly: You can take a seat, pick up a paddle, and catch a fish your first day on the water.

SINKs

Sit-in kayaks are best suited for bad weather. Anglers fishing the Extreme North will appreciate the protection from the elements that these boats offer. (Photo: Ken Shultz)

Still, there are a few anglers plying the water in SINKs. Those who use them, love them. Guys who paddle 20 miles to catch a fish are die-hard sit-in fans. Guys who fish in brutal weather also love their sit-ins. In fact, kayak anglers who come to the sport from kayaking will have a hard time getting out of their SINKs. It's like trading in a Corvette for a Chevette. In fact, several manufacturers include sit-in models in their fishing lineup.

SINKs are sleek and fast. Since you're actually sitting below the waterline, the boat can have a narrow keel that will reduce water resistance and improve efficiency. Moreover, you can get more paddle in the water, increasing torque and power. Many SINK loyalists also note that the available deck space offers more options for mounting electronics and gear within easy reach. Even more important, the

SINK's hull protects your legs from the elements, keeping you warmer, drier, and out of the sun.

For most kayak anglers, however, the sit-in's disadvantages outweigh its good points. The biggest problem is that SINKs just aren't as safe as SOTs. If you flip over in a sit-in kayak, you have to know how to either turn the boat back over while still stuck in the cockpit—called an Eskimo roll—or get out of the boat while submerged, aka wet exit. Then, once the boat is righted, you must know how to empty the water and get back into the cockpit. That's a lot of know-how. Before paddling a sit-in, it is highly recommended that a 'yaker take a paddle course that will teach these lifesaving skills. Sit-ins are even difficult to get in and out of on dry land. Launching and landing require you to bend yourself into unnatural positions just to fit inside the cockpit. Also, the tight hull has a tendency to make some paddlers feel claustrophobic; it even causes blisters and bruises where the boat rubs against your skin. Unless you're an experienced paddler, it is widely recommended that you enter the sport in a SOT. For that reason, this book will focus on choosing, rigging, and using a sit-on-top. Still, most of the information will apply to either type of boat.

Kayak Shapes and Styles

Kayaks come in many shapes and styles, but most sit-on-tops targeted to fishermen share some basic features. There will be a forward hatch in the bow, flat surfaces on the deck, a cockpit with foot wells and a seat, a raised center section with cup holders and flat areas for gear, scupper holes to drain water from the cockpit, a tank well to store gear behind the seat, handles for carrying the boat, and a drain plug to release water from inside the hull. Some boats may also come with a bungee cord for storing the paddle, deck loops to affix gear, or even a rudder.

You'll find a lot of diversity when it comes to hull shape. Each manufacturer has its own unique hull design that offers specific advantages for specific types of fishing. For surf launching, you'll want a boat that has a sharp entry and broader stern to punch through the waves. Kayak fishermen who are looking to stand and fish will want a boat that puts its width in the middle to support sight casting. Many anglers use their kayak as a floating tacklebox while they wade an area of shallow water. These folks need a smaller, lighter boat that won't drag through the water and hold them back while they walk the flats.

Whatever the intended use, the main objectives in hull design are efficiency and maneuverability—getting the most forward momentum out of each paddle stroke, and turning with little effort. The main objectives in cockpit design are ergonomics and function—fishing in comfort and control. Each manufacturer has its own way of approaching these objectives, while each angler will have individual requirements for meeting them.

The Hull Truth

To better understand kayak design, talk to someone who designs kayaks. Allen Stancil cooks up boats for Liquidlogic Kayaks in North Carolina. He's put together everything from whitewater to open-ocean kayaks, winning awards for his cutting-edge designs. Lately, Stancil has been pouring his talents into the company's new line of fishing kayaks, making him more than qualified to explain some terms important to understanding kayak design.

When considering the hull of a prospective fishing kayak, several elements deserve close attention. First, the bow. According to Stancil, the front of the boat should be relatively wide so that it will ride over waves and not dig in or plow through. The bow should also push spray out to the side, keeping 'yak and 'yaker dry. An effective bow will carry the boat up and over the waves, allowing it to ride on its keel and glide through the water.

The shape of the boat's stern is as important as the shape of the bow. Stancil suggests you look for a boat that has a sharp tail section as opposed to a rounded stern. "Water wants to stick to a round edge," he points out, "which increases drag." The section of the stern where the keel comes up to the back of the boat and off the side, called the *stem*, should be a sharp angle in order to release water and

For big-water paddling, look for a kayak that has a pronounced bow flare to defend against spray, a sharp entry to cut through the waves, a pronounced chine to offer stability, and a large bow hatch to store rods.

avoid hydraulic boiling and rooster-tailing. The bow and the stern work together to rise over the waves then release the water, enabling you to glide along with the least amount of effort.

One of the most important elements of a kayak's hull is its *rocker*—the bend in the keel from bow to stern. To test rocker, place the kayak on a flat surface and push down on the stern. The rocker is the point where the boat teeters backward. The placement and angle of the rocker determines how a boat will handle under way. Stancil explains that a boat featuring a dramatic bend from bow to stern will push water, not glide through it. A boat that is flat on the bottom won't track well and it will be more difficult to turn. A perfectly placed rocker allows you to lean to one side or the other to make slight adjustments in the boat's course. You can paddle steady and stay straight without having to take extra strokes to turn the boat. This is because a well-designed rocker allows you to lean to one side, causing the boat to travel on its chine, not its keel.

Chine and keel help the boat track properly and determine its stability. *Tracking* is the kayak's tendency to travel in a straight line. The *keel* is the edge that runs down the center of the hull; the *chine* is the angle at which the keel rises to the side of the boat. A hard chine and sharp keel allow the boat to lean and steer, while a flat bottom and soft chine keep the boat steady but make it less maneuverable.

The shape of the keel and the angle of the chine also play a big part in the boat's stability. At first glance, a kayak that has a sharp keel and hard chine would seem less stable than a boat that has a flat keel and softer chine. But it isn't that obvious. Stancil points out that a boat has two types of stability. *Primary stability* is the kayak's tendency to stay upright when you're sitting straight. As you lean to one side, however, the boat also leans to one side until it catches and stops— this is *secondary stability*. The harder the chine and the sharper the keel, the less primary stability a boat has. On the other hand, a boat with a flatter bottom and softer chine will have plenty of primary stability but be less nimble.

To test stability, take the boat for a paddle in warm, shallow water and lean it from one side to the other until it catches. The easier it leans and the faster it goes over, the quicker the boat will be. The key is to have confidence in the secondary stability. Even if the boat feels like it's going to flip at any moment, as long as it has plenty of secondary stability you won't end up in the drink.

But stability is more than just your chances of falling overboard; it has everything to do with the way the boat handles. Oddly enough, if you're planning on plying rough waters you'll be looking for *less* primary stability. Stancil explains that primary stability wants to keep the boat flat while the waves want to make it rock. A kayaker paddling a stable kayak through rough water will work harder than one paddling a more responsive craft. Strange, but true.

Rocker, chine, and keel are key to a kayak's performance. A boat that has a hard chine, balanced rocker, and sharper keel will be more responsive, yet less stable, than a boat with softer features. "The beginning paddler is going to pick a boat that feels stable," Stancil says, "but in a year he'll realize he's paddling a slug."

Tandems

Some kayak anglers hope to kill two birds with one stone. Instead of buying a separate kayak for their spouse and themselves, they get the bright idea to buy a tandem and "fish together." The family that fishes together, stays together, right? Wrong. The family that fishes in a tandem kayak together usually ends up killing each other.

Two people swinging hooks and heavy lead while sitting on a little piece of plastic is a disaster waiting to happen. A husband and wife attempting to navigate a kayak is a divorce waiting to happen. Tandems might be fun for touring or if a parent wants to take a child on the water, but if you want to introduce another adult to the joys of kayak fishing . . . buy another kayak.

Pedal Power!

One of the challenges of kayak fishing is maneuvering the boat while fishing at the same time. Paddling with one arm and fishing with the other is possible—although awkward. Attempting this can make 'yak anglers wish they were born with four arms. Until evolution catches up with the sport, we'll have to settle for fishing *or* paddling, but not both.

Enter Hobie Cat with one of the most innovative kayaks to hit the fishing scene. The Hobie Mirage uses a pedal system to flap two fin-shaped paddles under the boat. These flippers propel the boat at a good clip and free up your hands for fishing. The boat is steered with a lever that you use to control a rudder in the stern. Since the Mirage will not go in reverse, the boat comes equipped with an auxiliary paddle for tight turns and going backward.

Cockpit Layout

Stancil's skills as a kayak designer extend to the top side of the boat, too. He is as careful about laying out the cockpit as he is about carving the hull. "Everything has a purpose," he says, and attention is paid to every detail.

Out of all the carefully designed elements in a kayak, Stancil admits, "The seat is the most important part." Anyone who has spent time paddling will agree. Even the toughest angler will be humbled by a sore butt. It's one of the facts of the game. So Stancil looks for a boat with a seat that's higher than the foot wells. Elevating the butt above the heels facilitates good blood circulation, keeping your legs, feet, and rear from going numb. Moreover, the seat area should have good drainage to allow water to drain away from your skin. Sitting in a puddle all day is very uncomfortable. Whether a boat is designed with a backrest built in or set up to accept an aftermarket seat, choose a model that will be comfortable over the long haul. Any weakness in seat design will not be evident until it is too late—when you're miles from home with an aching back, cramped legs, and a screaming ass.

Another integer in the comfort equation is the *foot wells*—the indentions that run on either side of the console to hold your legs and feet. Together with the seat, the foot wells can make or break a kayak. They should do two things: support your feet and legs, and drain water from the boat. Since most kayakers paddle with their legs bent at the knees and their heels resting on the floor of the foot wells, the kayak should have something for the feet to rest on. Some boats have adjustable pegs sticking out of each side of the well; others feature raised ridges to support the heel. First-time kayakers don't realize how important the legs are to paddling (more on that later), but an effective foot well will greatly increase both comfort and paddling power.

The foot wells are also the main channels for water to drain from the boat. They should be angled down to the *scuppers*—the holes molded through the boat for drainage—so that water quickly runs away from you and out of the boat. In addition to the foot wells, most boats have scuppers under the seat and in the tank well. These holes should be high enough above the waterline that they do not allow water in when the boat is loaded down. Oddly enough, water running into the scuppers is a common occurrence with fishing kayaks—most boats actually require scupper plugs to close up the holes and keep the water out. Which, of course, defeats the purpose of the scuppers in the first place. Again, the effectiveness of the scupper, seat, and foot wells will not be evident until the boat is thoroughly water-tested.

Other qualities, though, will be immediately evident. Stancil, like most fishing kayak designers, tries to lay out his boats to suit each angler's individual needs and preferences. "The tank well should be large enough for an office crate or a scuba tank," he says, "and include plenty of flat surfaces to mount rod holders and electronics." He also adds recessed nooks and crannies within easy reach to hold the flotsam and jetsam of fishing: sinkers, hooks, jigs, pliers, bait, and so on. "Everything's flush," Stancil continues. "Cleats, bungees, even carrying handles should be below the level of the deck so lines don't get caught." Most boats feature a bungee cord to hold the paddle to the side of the hull when it's not being used, along with other cords stretched across the hatches or wells to keep loose gear in place. There should also be a handle on the bow and one on the stern, along with a strap on each side to carry or drag the boat. Cleats and metal eyes should be installed in convenient places for you to tie and clip gear to the hull. These amenities should be scattered around the boat, since most kayakers don't realize their value until they need them.

Hatches

Hatches are another standard kayak item that has no standard—they come in different sizes and shapes, though all achieve the same goal. In fact, the hatch is the weakest link on the boat. After all, a hatch is nothing more than a gaping hole in the top of the kayak. Not all hatches are created equal, and kayak designers seem to wrestle with the hatch problem, solving the dilemma in different ways.

Obviously, having a big hole in the top of the boat is a problem. Yet dry storage is premium on a kayak, so hatches are a necessary evil. Sealing a hatch is not a science—they all leak, some more than others. The cover should be tight enough to keep water out, but loose enough to let you into the boat. All hatches should have straps or at least bungees over the top to keep them from popping off.

Many companies even attach the hatch cover to the boat with a tether to keep it from falling overboard and drifting away.

Most boats have at least a bow hatch. This opening should be big enough to allow you to store fishing rods inside the boat. The bow hatch should have a raised edge—higher than the top of the deck—that the hatch cover fits on tightly. Rubber covers that stretch over the hatch like a Tupperware lid are not reliable—the slightest pressure from within the boat or wind or wave could break the hatch loose and leave an open hole in the kayak. Very bad. If you have one of these covers, always attach a tether to keep it with the boat, and use straps or bungees to keep it on the boat. Don't trust it. Even the best hatches aren't perfect. Despite their great efforts, kayak designers have yet to come up with the completely waterproof hatch. On a kayak, "dry storage" should really be called "damp storage."

In addition to a bow hatch, some boats have smaller access points in the cockpit—usually between your legs or behind the seat. These holes should be covered tightly with a screw-on top. The small, round compartments usually have some sort of removable cup or bag recessed inside to hold small items. Stancil points out that on his latest kayak, he made the cups from hard white plastic so that paddlers can easily see what's inside.

Besides providing damp storage, hatches are also the only way that you can get to the inside of a sit-on-top kayak. Mounting rod holders, fishfinder transducers, and batteries may require you to tinker around belowdeck. Make sure the hatches are large enough and appropriately located to give you access to the inside of the boat, yet tightly sealed to keep water out.

Capacity

Even though each kayak manufacturer lists a weight capacity for its boats, not every kayak company uses the same formula to come up with this number. What is "capacity"? The weight at which the boat handles best? The weight at which water comes up through the scuppers? The weight at which the boat will sink? Truth is, capacity could be any of these qualities.

When choosing a kayak, many anglers—especially big guys—look at the boat's capacity first and other features second. For good reason. Still, given the importance of design and the ambiguity of the listed capacity, weight limit is just another factor in a long list of them. There are plenty of 6-foot-plus, 250-pound-plus anglers paddling 10- and 12-foot kayaks, and an equal number of little guys cruising around in 15- and 16-footers. A plus-sized angler who'll spend most of his time weaving in and out of backwater creeks or small farm ponds doesn't have to give up maneuverability to gain capacity. Likewise, minus-sized anglers who will cover long distance across open water can handle a longer, more seaworthy boat. Problems will arise, however, if the plus-sized guy tries to paddle into the open ocean in his little boat. He will most likely find the boat very unstable and constantly filling with water. Likewise, if the diminutive angler takes his big boat into the Outback, he'll have to work very hard to navigate around turns and through structure. Be sure to look beyond just capacity when you're purchasing your boat: A fishing kayak should fit not only you, but also the type of fishing you intend to do.

Color

Kayaks come in as many colors as they do sizes and configurations. Although it may seem that the color of your kayak is purely a personal choice, in fact other factors come into play when you think about where and how you'll use the boat. If you fish areas with heavy boat traffic, a brighter color will be a lifesaver. If you fish in bright sunlight, a darker boat will cut down on glare. Some 'yaks double as hunting platforms, making dark green or tan a good choice. Jeez, even picking the color is hard!

Kicking Tires

Kayak qualities such as handling and comfort will only be evident after a thorough test paddle. Most reputable outfitters will be happy to transport a selection of kayaks to a local watering hole for a prospective customer to compare. Even better, many paddle shops offer kayak fishing clinics, classes, and even guided trips where folks new to the sport can test the waters before diving in headfirst. Once you're out on the water, make the best of the demo ride by checking the following items:

Test-Paddle Checklist

• **Get in the kayak.** Load it with rods and tackleboxes. Do the boxes fit in the tank well? Do the rods fit in the forward hatch? Push the boat into the water about ankle-deep and climb on top. How easy is it to get in? Does the boat tip or rock excessively?

• **Get comfortable.** Adjust the seat and foot pegs to fit your body. Do the rods or tackleboxes get in the way? How easy is it to adjust the seat and foot pegs from inside the kayak? Best bet: Buy the most comfortable seat you can afford and test it in each prospective kayak.

• **Get going.** From a complete stop, take a few strokes of the paddle. How easily does the boat come up to speed? Liquidlogic's Allen Stancil says that a kayak should reach gliding speed after four strokes. How hard do you have to paddle to get going? Does the boat feel sluggish? Best bet: Buy the lightest/strongest paddle that you can afford and use it on the test paddle.

• **Get settled.** Once you're on the water, comfortable, and up to speed, paddle a mile or more in a straight line. How well does the boat stay on course? How much effort is required to keep the boat up to speed? How much water comes over the sides and bow of the boat? Does the paddle hit the gunnels of the boat on the down-stroke? After half a mile, you should forget that you're paddling. After a mile, how do your legs, arms, butt, and back feel? Is it love?

• **Handling.** Find a bridge piling, buoy, or channel marker and make a hard turn around it. Spin the boat in place. Paddle in reverse. Spin the boat in reverse. Take off quickly. Stop abruptly. How's it feel?

• **Chop, chop.** If you'll be using your kayak on open water, do not make a decision without paddling in rough conditions. It's important to experience how the boat rises or cuts through the waves when it really counts. How much water comes over the bow? Does it drain quickly? Does water puddle in the seat, foot wells, hatches, tank well? If choppy conditions aren't available, at least cut across some boat wakes to get an idea of the hull's ability to handle the rough stuff.

• **Whoa, Nelly.** In calm, shallow, warm water, test the kayak's stability. Lean to one side as far as possible. Quickly switch sides. How fast does the boat respond? Rock back and forth. Does the boat tilt awkwardly? Sit sideways in the cockpit with your legs over the side. Sit backward. Stand up. Kneel. Scoot up to the bow and open the hatch. Simulate the worst possible stability situations to see how the boat responds.

• **Get loaded.** Return to the launch and empty the boat. Drag it across the sand. Lift it by each handle. Carry it a couple dozen yards. Does it fit on top of the car? Will it fit in the garage?

The importance of a test ride cannot be stressed too highly. Without trying several different models, an inexperienced paddler will have nothing to compare a new boat with. Advice from experts, pros, and outfitters is jaded—we all love our kayaks after we've dropped a grand on 'em. When I went looking for my first 'yak, I was dead set on a particular boat. I liked the color. I even tested the boat and, although I thought it was sluggish, since I didn't have any other experience, I almost bought it. But a colleague insisted that I try another model. An ugly color. Just to be sure, I splashed the second boat. Love at first stroke. Now I like the color.

Choosing a kayak is not a decision that should be based on one factor or another, but on all of them weighed together. Even though each model will have pluses and minuses, one kayak's pluses will outweigh the minuses. One kayak will compensate for your weak points and accentuate your strengths. One kayak will let you paddle to the places you want to go and catch the fish you want to catch. That's the one. That's your new best friend.

2

Kayak Rigging the Right Way

If picking out a kayak is the hard part, rigging it is the fun part. Even after you've purchased an appropriate boat, there's still much work to be done. From buying the basics—seat, paddle, PFD—to adding bells and whistles like electronics, a rudder, and rod holders, it's time to build your kayak into a custom fish-catching machine.

Understand, kayak anglers are like all anglers: If there's something that can help us catch fish *we must have it.* We're suckers for any gizmo that might give us an edge against our naked adversary. Bait wells, fishfinders, VHF, GPS—if anglers have it, we want it. And with a little ingenuity, we can have it, too. Likewise, any advantage in kayak speed, comfort, or efficiency is also a must-have. Carbon-fiber paddles, gel seats, and purpose-built PFDs are required equipment for any serious paddler.

Whether you're an insatiable tinkerer or a store-buying pragmatist, kayak fishing offers the freedom to build the boat of your dreams. I am of the latter class, having neither the time nor the will (not to mention the ability) to build much of anything. I'd rather buy the latest gadget, slap it on my 'yak, and go fishing. Other anglers find joy in do-it-yourself kayak rigging, spending hours bent over their boats like mad scientists, bringing impossible creations to life.

Luckily for the rigging-inept, countless companies now offer every bell and whistle imaginable shrink-wrapped with step-by-step instructions. Kayak fishing's popularity has spawned a scourge of companies turning out everything from purpose-built milk crates to prepackaged anchor systems. Accessories that were once the product of the DIY workshop are now available at every brick-and-mortar paddle shop and online cyber merchant.

But there is still plenty of opportunity to create for the creative. Drills, saws, snips, torches, rivet guns, and putty knives are the tools of the kayak surgeons who cut, punch, poke, and melt their boats into one-of-a-kind fishing craft. Even items that can be purchased are often better made. And there is always the satisfaction of personalizing a boat to reflect your own personality. No two kayakers and no two kayaks are alike.

A Word About $

One theme will permeate this chapter: *Don't skimp.* Whether you're buying the basics, the bells and whistles, or the boat itself—get the best stuff money can buy. Of course, some kayak anglers are kayak anglers because motorboats are cost-prohibitive. But precisely because you don't have to worry about gas, oil, maintenance, and storage with a kayak, you shouldn't worry about spending a few extra bucks when it comes to outfitting that boat. Moreover, kayak angling is tough on both angler and the kayak—cheap stuff just won't hold up. Cutting corners on the initial rigging of the boat will catch up with you down the line when things break and need replacing. And if things break out on the water, when you need them the most, the cost could be a lot higher than a few extra bucks. So purchase the best equipment possible, from a reputable paddle shop, and have it installed by an experienced kayak engineer. Because when you're out in the middle of nowhere chasing a trophy fish, the only two things you can rely on are your boat and your strength. Only one of those things can be bought. Don't skimp!

The Basics

A fully rigged kayak is a plastic battle wagon with heavy rods for big fish, a Crate Mate Jr. for heavy tackle, PFD, VHF, GPS, Scotty, and flush-mounted rod holders all on Wheeleez wheels ready to roll.

Before leaving the shop with your new kayak, you'll need three things: a seat, a paddle, and a personal flotation device. Each is essential to comfort and safety. Even the best kayak will be worthless without a top-quality seat and high-powered propulsion system. And the best kayaker will be worthless without an effective PFD.

I remember the day I bought my first 'yak. My friendly neighborhood paddle outfitter suggested strongly that I invest in a high-quality paddle, seat, and PFD. I took one look at the price tag and said, "I'm not paying that much for a stick and a couple of pieces of foam!" So I went with "entry-level" models. Six months later I was in the store buying a new top-of-the-line paddle; a year after that I was buying the best-you-can-get seat. In a short time—of unabashed abuse—I had blown all the stitches out of my seat and warped my paddle to the point that it rattled with every stroke. Trying to save a few bucks up front cost me twice as much in the long run.

I abuse my stuff, totally disrespect it. I drag, drop, crash, and grind my boat, and I expect it to take all this and ask for more. That's one of the cool things about a fishing kayak—it's plastic, it's indestructible (almost). So your accessories should be indestructible, too. When launching through the surf or dragging through the backwaters, the last thing you want to worry about is busting something and having to limp home. A little investment up front will pay off in the long run.

Paddle

Would you put a trolling motor on a 40-foot sportfishing boat? Would you drive a Corvette with a four-cylinder engine? Would you fly in an F-18 fighter jet with propellers? Then why would you use a cheap paddle on a fishing kayak?

The design of the paddle is just as important as the design of the kayak. Using a crappy paddle on a good kayak is like putting a lawn mower engine in a nitro-burning funny car—stupid.

To get smart about kayak paddles, talk to a guy who builds them. Ed Vater is the president of Bending Branches, one of the most respected paddle manufacturers in the industry. "Paddles come in three price points," he explains. "Low-end paddles cost about $50, midrange paddles run $100, and high-end paddles will cost around $250." Each level of kayak paddle offers distinctive advantages over the level below it, meaning that the most expensive paddle will be the best paddle money can buy.

"For $50," Vater says, "you get two blades and a shaft." Most low-end paddles have a heavy aluminum shaft and flat plastic blades. He adds, "It'll work, but you won't have any fun." Moving up to the next level gets you a fiberglass or carbon-fiber shaft and molded plastic blades. "If you're going from A to B, spending at least a hundred bucks will get you a pretty good paddle," Vater says. He suggests you take a close look at the paddle's ferrule—the joint where its two halves come together. "If it clicks and rattles, that's really annoying—you're not having an enjoyable experience." You can also judge the quality of a paddle by its precision-ground ferrule. The two halves should not only fit together tightly, but stay tight over time under extreme duress. Cheap paddles may start out with a snug fit but will quickly bend and loosen with use. With a $100-class paddle, you get a composite shaft and precision ferrule—minimum requirements for a kayak angler.

Stepping up to the next level and purchasing a $250 paddle is like going from a Chevette to a Corvette. Sure, you drove that old four-banger around for years of reliable transportation, but when your fingers wrapped around the leather steering wheel and your foot stepped on 505 horsepower, there was no going back. It's the same with kayak paddles. "The bottom line," according to Vater: "You have to try it to know the difference." The extra money pays for space-age materials like carbon fiber and high-tech manufacturing techniques. This reduces the paddle's *swing weight*—its weight as it moves through the air. "Everyone worries about the paddle blade as it move through the water," Vater notes, "but the blade spends half the time moving through the air." A lighter paddle will move with less resistance, which reduces fatigue and allows you to go farther with less energy. When you figure that a top-quality paddle weighs up to a third less than a midrange product, and that you'll make more than 800 strokes when paddling 1 mile, the extra weight of a cheap paddle really adds up.

A good paddle also has a highly refined blade design. A low-end model will have a flat blade, while a high-end unit is shaped to move through the water smoothly. "Take a flat piece of paper and drop it, and it will flutter through the air," Vater says to illustrate the difference, "but crease the paper and drop it and it falls to the ground smoothly." The same concept applies to paddles. Each blade has a dihedral design—a slight crease down the center of its broad side. This allows it to move through the water without fluttering. If you're using a cheap paddle, you'll have to grip tightly and adjust the swing of your arms to fight the vibration of the blades. A sweet paddle, on the other hand, moves through the water with little effort and a consistent motion, reducing fatigue and increasing power. Using a Bending Branches Breeze paddle with the Day blade, I can maintain the momentum of my kayak with near-effortless paddle strokes. Moreover, I can adjust my grip, even paddling with only my fingers, which keeps blisters from forming on my hands. Vater has noticed that "Most sit-on-top kayak anglers prefer a shorter, wider blade because it's more powerful." Anglers will also want to choose a brightly colored paddle blade for added visibility on the water. "You can see bright blades over a mile away," Vater says, "but with neutral-color blades, visibility is reduced to a quarter mile." His company's Angler-model paddle comes with high-vis blades in either orange or yellow, and a measuring stick embossed on the shaft—just what the 'yak angler needs.

Once you've settled on a price point and chosen a paddle model, you'll have to choose a shaft of the correct length. "With sit-in kayaks, we consider the paddler's height and paddling style," Vater explains, "but with sit-on-tops it's all crap." Sit-in kayakers argue about blade width and aerodynamics—"but a SOT is a wide hog, so none of that really matters." SINK anglers will find a sizing chart on the Bending Branches Web site; SOT anglers, says Vater, should "just get a paddle that is long enough that you're not banging your knuckles on the hull." He recommends a 240-centimeter shaft for most SOT paddlers, though more experienced 'yakers may want a shorter paddle—down to 225 cm—that keeps the blade closer to the boat, reducing swing weight and increasing digging power.

According to Vater, outfitters often report a steady stream of paddlers returning a few months after buying their first kayak to purchase a top-of-the-line paddle. Put simply, "A good paddle makes for an enjoyable experience." That's what kayak anglers are doing on the water in the first place—having an enjoyable experience. Let me tell you, when a school of aggressive fish rises to the surface, busting and breaking in a frenzy of whitewater, and I dig in—my paddle accelerating with authority—chase down the school, and hook up on my first cast . . . now, that's an enjoyable experience.

Personal Flotation Device

Back in the day, I used to race mountain bikes. I always wore my helmet—it provided me with a false sense of security that allowed me to talk myself into some crazy stunts. My logic as I studied a steep descent was: *Hmmmm, charging down this rocky mountainside looks pretty dangerous . . . luckily I've got my helmet on!* I feel the same way about my PFD. *Hmmmm, crossing that inlet through a cranking current and standing rip might not be such a good idea,* I think, *but I've got my PFD on, so I'm safe. Right?*

Truth is, nothing can prevent accidents from happening, and no one can expect the unexpected. Still, people who take extreme sports to the extreme must combine caution with precaution. A paddler must first avoid dangerous situations, and second be ready when danger raises its ugly head. Wearing a PFD will not keep you safe, but it will keep you safer.

The key to a PFD's effectiveness is wearing it—always. A life vest will not work if it's stuck in a hatch, jammed behind the seat, or even lying on your legs. A PFD must be on and properly latched to work. For example, two of my friends were fishing a rock island about 4 miles from the beach. They were anchored 25 feet apart, targeting tautog with chunks of crab. When one of them ran out of crabs, he asked his fishing partner to chuck him another. His buddy threw him a crab, but it went long, splashing down a couple of feet away and quickly swimming to safety. A second crab landed short, falling in the water just out of reach. The third crab hit the mark—literally—landing with its pointy shell stuck deep in the kayaker's knee. Yeouch! Nice catch. The sight of a live crab sticking out of his knee caused the angler to get woozy, teeter, pass out, and tumble into the water. His life jacket was jammed under his hatch cover. Luckily, the cold water brought him back to the real world and, with some help from his crab-chucking buddy, he was able to get back into the kayak and paddle to the beach.

Okay, no one expects to get stuck in the leg with a live crustacean. Everyone, however, should expect bad things to happen when bobbing around in a little plastic boat, surrounded by sharp objects, on unpredictable water. Because the angler in our story (who is a very experienced waterman) was fishing close to shore, he felt safe. But he wasn't. Now he gets the point—pardon the pun.

But the life vest's fishing features must first accommodate the US Coast Guard's requirements. "The Coast Guard is extremely anal when it comes to PFDs," explains Bill Kline, a lead PFD designer at Patagonia. "They won't let us put anything on the back of the vest: no D-rings or pockets, which might catch on something." Hey, it's good that they're anal when it comes to saving lives.

The first step in choosing a comfortable and effective PFD is finding one that the Coast Guard has approved. To determine whether the life vest is the real thing, check the big label in the back. There should be a stamp of Coast Guard approval along with sizing guidelines.

According to Kline, "A Type III PFD works well for fishing from a kayak." Since most kayak anglers won't take their boats down raging whitewater, most don't need the kind of PFD that will float them through the rapids while unconscious. Instead, kayak anglers are looking for a vest that is cool and comfortable and can be used with a high-backed seat. He suggests looking for a life vest with plenty of storage for things that you need often and those you'd need in an emergency. A good PFD features pockets designed to hold small tackleboxes or a safety strobe, D-rings for a whistle or line clippers, and straps to clip a VHF radio or pliers.

Dave Hadden of Patagonia's Lotus Designs takes Kline's suggestions and incorporates them into USCG-approved life vests. He says a good PFD should be well thought out, covering every detail to balance comfort, use, and safety. "A mesh back design with the flotation high on the back is more comfy for high-backed seats," he gives as an example. Foam acts as an insulator, so mesh will keep the paddler cooler. "Look for a vest made of 500-denier Cordura nylon," he suggests, "because it's the lightest fabric that resists abrasion and puncture by hooks." Since kayak anglers are often fishing in salt water, Lotus uses marine-grade corrosion-resistant zippers and fasteners. All the materials are UV-resistant so they don't break down after years of exposure to the sun. But the difference between a good vest and a

great vest is in the details. Taking the vest to extremes to save space
while maintaining safety, companies like Lotus use hand-skived foam.
"That means we carve each piece of foam by hand," Hadden
explains, "so that it fits tightly within the nylon shell." This allows
them to meet Coast Guard standards *and* comfort standards by putting the most foam in the least space.

Once you've chosen a comfortable vest, it's time to figure out
the fit. Hadden instructs paddlers to look to the Coast Guard label in
each PFD. "First, make sure that the intended use on the label
matches the activity." Then look to the named size: small, medium,
large, or extra-large. Each size will cover a range of chest measure-
ments. With a tape, measure around the chest going under the arms
and over the shoulder blades. "Take into account undergarments,"
Hadden reminds paddlers; "the PFD should have room to tighten
down in the summer and loosen up in the winter." When making the
fine adjustments, Hadden again looks to the USCG label, where specific instructions are given for fit. "The PFD should be fastened and
secured," he says. "You really put yourself at risk with a loose vest."

Which pretty much sums up the point about life vests: There is
already plenty of inherent risk associated with kayak fishing. Why
make the sport more dangerous by not using the appropriate safety
equipment and taking all possible caution? Now, that would be
really stupid.

Seats

For first-time paddlers, the kayak's seat is probably the most often-
overlooked accessory. This mistake becomes painfully obvious on the
first outing. Yes, a badly designed boat will float. Yes, a poorly
designed paddle will push you along. Yes, a bulky, ill-fitting PFD may
even save your life. But an uncomfortable seat will cripple the
strongest paddlers, even if they're using the best equipment.

Anglers just getting into kayaking often don't realize the importance of a high-quality seat. Jason Smallwood at Surf to Summit—
the largest maker of top-quality seats and accessories—explains, "A
good kayak seat provides comfort and support." When you consider

that you'll spend hours in the seat, performing the same repetitive paddle stroke thousands of time over—it is easy to understand how important these two qualities are. A seat should not only be comfortable, but also give you support to do the dirty work of kayaking.

"It's not a lounge chair," Smallwood notes; "you don't want to lean back." Instead, you should lean slightly forward at the shoulders, your legs bent at the knee and your feet solidly supported by pegs or steps in the foot well. Many people think that the power in a paddle stroke comes from the arms. In fact, much of the energy comes from the lats, and even the gluts as your body twists to make each stroke. Your legs work, too, bracing you in the boat and counterbalancing the powerful push and twist required to stroke. An effective seat is key to supporting your lower back so that your mid-back can do the work. The seat back should not flex or give, allowing you to put your full power into each stroke without losing any effort to the bend of the backrest. The seat should be both stiff enough to support you and soft enough to absorb your spine's push against the hard plastic of the kayak. Mostly, it should be tough—built to take all the stretching, pushing, pulling, and twisting that a kayak angler can dish out.

"We make a lot of different types of seats," Smallwood points out, "because not every paddler is the same." Just as there are many different paddles, boats, and PFDs, there are seats to fit each kayaker's style and personality. A short paddler will want a shorter seat that doesn't interfere with his paddle stroke, while a taller 'yaker will want a taller seat that provides more support higher on her long spine.

Still, this general guideline for fit doesn't take into account comfort, which is entirely personal. The same seat that pleases one kayaker could put another, similar paddler in traction. One important thing to look for is padding—the amount as well as its placement on the seat. There should be plenty in the tailbone area. When you sit in one position for a long time, all your weight is transferred through your tailbone to the seat. This grating of bone on flesh on plastic will cause your back, butt, and legs to ache. Eventually, your feet may begin to tingle and go numb.

Even the best seat will be better with some extra padding in the base. You can find a variety of paddling pads that will pick up where the kayak seat leaves off. Whether it's a fancy gel pad or a chunk of closed-cell foam available at hardware stores, a seat pad will not only provide extra comfort, but also keep your butt out of any water that may collect under the seat.

Unlike paddles or PFDs, there is no formula for seat comfort. No matter how much "natural" padding you carry, bones rubbing on skin will eventually cause excruciating pain. The problem with choosing a seat is that its true qualities will not be evident until you've spent hours in the kayak on the water. Testing a seat in the kayak shop is impossible.

"Every seat will not fit every person," Smallwood admits. "That's why research is number one." He recommends that kayakers attend breakout days at their local paddle shop to put different seats in different boats, then put the whole system to the test on the water.

"It's not only comfort and support," he explains; "it's versatility." Many paddlers use different seats in different boats. A high back intended for a long, touring SOT that provides support for distance paddling will not be appropriate in a shorter backwater boat that needs to be maneuvered around tight turns.

Once you've found a comfortable seat, stick with it. Smallwood says that many 'yakers take their seat with them when they travel. He points to this as one advantage of Surf to Summit's fishing seat, which is outfitted with rod holders and a tackle bag: "Anywhere an angler goes, he can rent a kayak and have a fishing kayak."

Not only should a kayak seat be comfortable and offer support, it should also be tough. It will undergo incredible stresses as you paddle it and also when you transport and store it. Be sure that all seat components are of the highest quality. Clips and straps should be unbreakable. All seams should be stitched multiple times all the way through. The seat should be made of indestructible UV-resistant cloth. Expect it to offer solid support whether you're paddling steadily or leaning back hard to make an abrupt turn. It should also take the abuse of riding on the roof of a car at high speeds and being dropped, squashed, and twisted at home.

Even the perfect seat will need to be adjustable. A position that's comfortable at the beginning of a trip may be excruciating by the end. Many paddlers relieve fatigue by adjusting the seat as they paddle to shift their weight and position. An inch forward or back can do wonders to take stress off one set of muscles and place it on another. In kayaking, repeating the same action over and over for hours will wear muscles down. Changing position changes the angle that each muscle works. Look for straps and buckles that are easy to manipulate under pressure. A high-backed seat should have adjustments for the lower back and upper back. A kidney seat should have a thick strap to offer extra support across the lower back.

Whatever position you paddle in, the seat must be uncompromising—giving solid, reliable support against the intense pressure exerted by water and muscles. Believe it or not, the seat does as much to propel the kayaker as the paddle or boat does.

I usually paddle long distances with my back straight and my shoulders forward. When I arrive at the fishing grounds, I'll recline my seat slightly to allow more freedom of movement. While fishing, I pay close attention to my position in the seat, sitting up, leaning back, hanging my leg over the side of the boat, crossing my legs, even stretching my legs and back to keep from cramping.

Constantly changing the seat's position—even slightly—during the fishing trip will allow you to go farther and fish longer. A good seat will allow for an infinite number of positions to increase comfort and improve paddling power.

Electronics

Whoever first noted that "Necessity is the mother of invention" must have been a kayak angler. Getting all the gear and gizmos necessary for fishing onto a kayak takes a lot of invention. In the infancy of kayak fishing, anglers would take existing boats and cut, drill, and mold them into fishing kayaks. Thanks to the sweat and ingenuity of these early visionaries, modern kayak anglers have a slew of accessories available to them.

Not only are there now plenty of purpose-built kayak fishing goodies out there, but the early kayak pioneers solved most of the problems of bastardizing existing products for use in a kayak. Installing fishfinders, live wells, and rod holders is easy these days after the trial-and-error experiments of those first kayak anglers. Today most manufacturers of boating accessories have even solved these problems and are prepared to help their customers use the toys they make in any type of boat.

In fact, modern electronics offer so much power, in such a small package, that kayak anglers have an unimaginable range of tools available to them. Features and functions that were the exclusive realm of professional sportfishermen a few years ago are now available in a handheld unit for a couple hundred bucks. Moreover, the installation and operation of electronics that used to call for an electrical engineer and computer technician now requires only a couple of AA batteries and the press of a button.

These are good times for fishermen and bad times for fish.

With more anglers chasing fewer fish, there is a fine line between accessory and necessity. Do you need a fishfinder or simply want one? Do you need GPS or just want it? Still, whether you're a salt-of-the-earth fisher or state-of-the-art rodsmith, certain accessories are necessities.

Fishfinder

One such accessory may be the fishfinder. It would be great, of course, if a fishfinder actually found fish. Instead it marks the water depth, showing a representation of the bottom along with any structure and fish that cross its sonar signal—blowing the cover on fish once you've found them.

Still, a fishfinder is a nice thing to have on a kayak. Whereas powerboaters will argue that fishfinders are a safety item required to stay in the channel and off the flats, kayak anglers face little danger of running aground at high speed. It can keep you out of trouble in the surf, though. When you're launching, returning to the beach, or fishing open-water shoals, the fishfinder will show you where the shallow water is and where the danger of breaking waves exists. To stay safe in the surf zone, you must keep one eye on the waves and one on the water depth. When the 'finder shows deep water in a slough, relax and plot your course; when it shows shallow water on the bar—paddle like hell!

But most anglers will never face breaking waves in their kayaks. For them, the fishfinder is a nice-to-have extra that can dramatically improve their catch rate. Obviously a view of the bottom and any fish that might be under the kayak is more than just helpful. A good bottom machine will not only identify depth contours such as drops and rises, and structure like reefs, wrecks, rock piles, grass, and deadfalls, but also indicate temperature breaks along a thermocline and even the hardness of the bottom. Add a water thermometer and the fishfinder can tell you where fish are most likely holding, saving you a lot of paddle strokes. Hmmm, a fishfinder is starting to sound like less of an accessory and more of a necessity.

When it comes to choosing a fishfinder for a kayak, the same considerations arise that guide the choice of any other kayak fishing accessory: ruggedness, high quality, ease of operation, and reliability.

A fishfinder is the toughest component on the kayak to install, maintain, and use. Exposing the unit's multiple electrical connections, coils of wire, rechargeable power source, computer chips, LCD screen, and buttons to sun, sand, salt water, and beatings from paddles, rods, legs, and fish is a recipe for failure. A good fishfinder will have to suffer to perform on a kayak.

For this reason, a kayak fishfinder should be of the highest quality. I burned through several $100 units before I invested in a top-of-the-line unit that has given me years of reliable performance. When you do the math, that means I spent $200 on garbage before I spent $200 on a nice fishfinder. I should have just spent $300 on a great unit!

For tips on choosing a great unit, look to a company that makes some of the best. Ted Gartner is a product specialist at Garmin, one of the top companies in the business. He suggests that the first step kayak anglers take when picking a fishfinder should be talking with the company that makes it. "If you're looking at a couple of different units," he says, "call the manufacturer and ask about installation to measure customer service and know if they are familiar with kayak stuff."

He also suggests that anglers pay close attention to the screen resolution. "Resolution is measured in pixels per inch," he explains; "the more pixels, the clearer the picture." A higher-resolution image will help you identify targets, discerning between structure and fish and even identifying specific types of fish that are holding below the kayak. "A lot of people think color is a bell and whistle," he adds, "but color makes the display easier to read at a moment's notice." He urges kayak anglers to use a unit with at least 160 pixels per inch. Another tip Gartner gives kayak anglers: "Take the unit out into the sunshine and see how it performs under natural light, not just in the showroom.

"You're selling yourself short," Gartner continues, "if you're sitting on a state-of-the-art kayak but can't read the fishfinder." The machine's screen should reduce glare and be easy to see even when you're wearing polarized sunglasses. A monochrome unit should be bright—employing a light gray background and dark black targets to increase contrast. A higher gray scale will also improve contrast within a target, allowing you to differentiate between fish and structure. Not only should the unit use high pixels to provide high contrast, but it should also have a large display. Kayakers don't often have the luxury of installing the unit within arm's reach and at eye level; you want a screen that's large enough to be seen from several feet away.

The best units, like Garmin's, also have a "see-through" feature that allows the sonar to separate weak signal returns, distinguishing fish from thermoclines, as well as a depth control gain that shows different levels of bottom hardness in varying shades of gray. A fishfinder should be sensitive enough that you can see fish swimming deep, differentiate between hard bottom and soft sand, and tell schools of bait from schools of big fish.

Looking beyond the display quality, your unit should also have easy-to-use features. Zoom, split screen, range, gain, and bottom lock should be quick to access and simple to turn on, turn off, and adjust. These features should be controlled by large, easy-to-use buttons—the fewer, the better. It should be a simple matter to transfer from zoom to normal view or adjust range and gain. The buttons should perform a variety of tasks without seizing up or falling off. Most important, the fishfinder's operation should be simple and straight-forward. You should be able to understand the operations performed by each function, and how to access each. Before buying a particular unit, thumb through the instruction book to see if it's organized and easy to understand. Many companies even offer step-by-step tutorials via CD or online. Operating the fishfinder shouldn't be like oper-ating the space shuttle; it should be an extension of your mind, like a third eye under the water.

Of course, a fishfinder is only as good as its *transducer*—the com-ponent that sends and receives the sound signals to identify the fish and structure under the boat. Several factors determine the effective-ness of the transducer: first power, and second signal. Power is meas-ured in kilohertz (kHz); most units use 50 kHz.

Another important consideration is installation. Not only should a kayak fishfinder be easy to set up, but it should be easy to put on and take off the boat. The transducer puck should be small enough to fit flat on the curved hull inside the kayak. The display unit should fit in a nook on the boat where it won't stick up and catch lines or take abuse. Since most anglers won't permanently mount the fishfinder's display unit, but take it off the boat at the end of each trip, the transducer's cable and mounting bracket should be quick to connect and release. The base should also allow for easy adjustment to change the angle of the fishfinder and reduce glare on the screen. Keep the connections snug, but not tight, to allow the unit to absorb the occasional accidental whack with a paddle or foot. Just like the unit, the bracket must be tough—capable of taking the abuse of crashing waves, flopping fish tails, and the sticks and stones of kayak fishing.

Take time in the showroom to run each prospective sonar through its paces. Push all the buttons, access all the features, examine the display, connect and disconnect the cables—spend some quality time with the unit before making a purchase. You want a unit that performs quickly, easily, and flawlessly under the most extreme conditions.

GPS

Depending on the type of kayaking you plan to do, a GPS could be an accessory or a necessity. For most types of kayaking, the addition of a global positioning system will lean toward the latter. GPS is a valuable tool to help you find fish, and an indispensable tool to help you find your way.

One of the advantages to fishing out of a kayak is that a kayak can go where no other boat can. A GPS will help you find hidden fishing destinations and get you home, too, without the assistance of a search party. Whether you'll be plying the boundless lakes and swamps of the Midwest or picking your way through the marshes and backwater bays on either coast, a GPS will steer you to more fishing holes and more fish.

As with the other equipment that you take aboard, the GPS will need to be high quality and easy to operate. Obviously, a kayak GPS must be waterproof and float. Ted Gartner at Garmin explains that there are different levels of waterproofing for marine electronics. Kayak anglers will want at least an IPX 7, which means the unit can be submerged at 1 meter for 30 minutes and still be expected to work. "If a kayaker is submerged for more than 30 minutes," Gartner jokes, "he's got more problems than his GPS."

True, but the real value of waterproofing comes not from holding the unit underwater, but from the constant exposure to liquid it gets in the course of a day on the water. Nothing in a kayak will stay dry—least of all the electronics that are mounted on the deck and constantly exposed to rain, snow, sleet, and drenching from waves and spray, even on a nice day. The "30-minute" standard is a mark of the unit's limit underwater but also, and more important, its susceptibility to eventually succumbing to exposure.

Choose a unit with the highest waterproof rating, because the GPS will only fail when it is needed, possibly stranding you far from shore, home, and safety. One spring my friends and I ventured out to Virginia's Eastern Shore to fish for bull red drum. Most of my companions abandoned the cause after lunch, leaving me and my best fishing buddy alone to fish the incoming tide. I had spent the paddle out to the fishing grounds carefully mapping the shoals with my GPS, identifying the deep water and laying a track for our return to the launch after dark.

The tide picked up late in the afternoon, and the bite picked up just before dark. Confident that our safe route home was saved on my GPS, we stayed past sunset and caught several big reds of better than 40 inches. After we'd had our fill, we pulled anchor and I turned on my GPS. Nothing. The screen was a mess of streaking lines and gibberish. The unit had been compromised—water had seeped in and my route was lost.

We had only the feeble rising moon and the ambient glow of the last rays of the setting sun to guide us through the dangerous shoals and breaking surf. We paddled back by Braille, feeling our way through the sloughs and bars and listening to the sound of crashing waves to warn us of impending disaster. Before we reached the deep bay on the back of the shoals, we had to cross one more bar. I heard my buddy yell, "Look out!" as a wave lifted us into the air, broke violently, and deposited both of us completely shaken in the deep water on the other side of the bar. Too close to chance again. I didn't even bother replacing the fizzled unit, just went out and bought the GPS with the highest IPX rating I could find.

Chances are that the GPS with the highest IPX will have the highest-quality features, too. The most important of these is a large, bright screen. Since you may have to mount the GPS at some distance from your seat, it's essential that the images on the screen are easy to see at a distance. At the least, the unit should have a high gray scale (number of shades of gray available), but a color finder is easiest to see. With a full-color image you can monitor your course, check your speed, and note the distance to a waypoint at a glance. "The human eye can recognize colors faster than gray," Garmin's Ted Gartner points out. "If you're in the middle of navigating, you can get info that is in color more quickly." When the conditions get rough, these features take on even more importance, allowing you to keep one eye on the waves and the other on your course.

A GPS shows you not only where you're going, but how fast you're going as well. This is an invaluable feature for kayak anglers. Paddling is a physical undertaking equal to pedaling a bicycle. Just as cyclists constantly monitor their pace and speed to maintain a consistent effort over a time and distance, you must avoid going so fast that your muscles bonk before you hit the beach. And if wind and current are slowing you to a crawl, a GPS will assure you that you're making progress. It's hard to determine your speed when you're paddling against wind and current a couple of miles offshore. This leads some paddlers to panic, put forth too much effort, and quickly burn out. If you can't line up two reference points (a tree and a telephone pole, for instance) and gauge your progress, then the speed function on the GPS is almost as important as the navigation features.

Even the best GPS is no replacement for a simple compass. No kayaker should be caught without at least a handheld or, better yet, a marine-grade compass mounted to the boat. Several models of sport compasses feature a wide-angle viewing area, allowing you to read the compass even as the boat is being rocked by waves. The compass should also have an anti-roll compensator to keep the dial steady in rough conditions. Look for a unit that mounts on a swiveling bracket so you can fold it away when it's not in use.

Of course, a GPS is as much a fishfinding tool as it is a safety tool, and it makes fishing easier as well as more fun. The most advanced GPS will zoom into an area 20 feet around, giving you incredible detail on your track and waypoints. A good GPS with high-resolution maps is the key to uncovering hidden fishing grounds. While trolling, the GPS will keep you moving at a constant speed. Using the map, you can trace back over your tracks to repeat a productive drift, or systematically crisscross an area looking for the bite. When a line goes down, you can mark the location of a school of fish with the push of a button. By using the GPS with a fishfinder, you can even mark the exact location of a wreck, drop, hump, or brush pile.

To get the most out of the unit, it must have buttons and features that logically control easy-to-understand menus. You shouldn't need a degree in computer science to work your GPS. The most often-used features should be available with one or two button pushes. Numbers and letters should be simple to type with a toggle in order to quickly input latitude and longitude numbers as well as names of waypoints. More important, the receiver should pick up satellite signals quickly—locking position within a minute of power-up and continually updating maps and data regardless of weather and overhead obstructions such as trees or bridges.

One of the most valuable features of a GPS is its computer interface. When you return home, you can hook your GPS into your computer and download the history of the day's trip. At that point you can rename waypoints, make notes on the bite, and log the distance you traveled and time on the water. Reviewing such information, you'll likely notice trends and patterns that may have affected the fish. As Garmin's Gartner puts it, "You can study data more carefully in your living room than you can when you're bobbing around in your boat."

There is no doubt that a GPS is a valuable tool for both navigating and fishing. It helps get you to and from the fishing grounds, as well as catching more fish while you're there. And paddling a kayak takes so much effort, any device that saves time and energy is more than an extra—it *is* a necessity.

VHF

Next to a PFD, a VHF radio is the most important safety item on a fishing kayak. Sure, a personal flotation device will keep you afloat, but a very high frequency radio will help rescuers find you. Like a PFD, a VHF will give you the courage to go farther and fish harder by providing a safety net should anything go wrong. A handheld radio is also a valuable tool for finding fish. You can call buddies in to the bite or eavesdrop on boaters and get the lowdown on the fishing action. A cell phone is not a substitute for a waterproof VHF. I never leave the launch without my radio clipped to my PFD.

I must admit, though, that I bought my VHF more for fishing than for safety. There were countless nights when my fishing buddy and I would get separated. I would search in vain for the bite then meet up with him later to find that he was tearing 'em up only a few hundred yards away. Or I'd show up at the launch late and discover I couldn't find my crew—and I had no way of contacting them. Many times I would be drifting along catching nothing, wondering if anyone was having better luck. With a quick call on the VHF, I can find out.

To target fish on the flats or around thick structure, strip down the kayak to the bare essentials—no crate, no lights, no electronics, no holders.

As with any other accessory, not all VHF radios are created equal. Some have more power than others, some are smaller than others, some are easier to use, some more reliable, and some VHF radios are just better. Again, a good indication of quality is price, but there are other factors, like size and features, that can bring the price down and

the quality up. On a kayak the VHF, like everything else, will be sub-
jected to inhuman torture. A high-quality model will last longer and
perform flawlessly when it really counts.

Most handheld VHFs use a rechargeable battery, but the best
have an adapter that will take standard AA batteries. Use the
rechargeable battery as the main battery, but always keep the AAs as
a backup. Even the best unit is worthless when the batteries die.

*A headlamp and navigation light make night fishing possible. The good
possibility of catching a big fish makes it desirable.*

Another thing to consider is the speaker. A good VHF will have a speaker face that can take constant dunking. VHFs usually have two power settings, 1 watt and 5 watts. The latter will give you more range, but the former will protect battery time. Often I cannot hear boaters who have their antennae mounted high off the water, but they can hear me. Moreover, the Coast Guard can usually pick up a handheld VHF miles away from its station.

Another invaluable benefit of the VHF is instant weather information. By monitoring any of the dedicated NOAA weather channels, the 'yaker can keep an ear on the weather beyond keeping an eye on the sky. When storm systems are in the area, I'll listen to buoy reports of wind speed to determine which direction and how fast a front is moving. NOAA weather radio also provides tidal information and weather bulletins.

I always feel safer with my VHF, so I always keep it clipped to my PFD—if I go over and lose my boat, I want to make sure I don't lose my VHF. Anytime you'll be venturing out farther than you can swim back, a radio is a must-have accessory.

With a palette of accessories, gadgets, and doohickeys, kayak anglers can turn their plastic canvas into a work of fishing art.

3

Safety

Kayaking is dangerous. So is walking down the street, watching television, and breathing air. Still, the latter activities don't necessarily invite danger but may encounter it—while the former almost asks for trouble. Climbing into a little boat powered by brute strength and raw determination, pushing away from the safety of terra firma, and paddling into the unpredictable world of water, wind, and waves is disaster waiting to happen. Although this scenario should repel rational people, it actually attracts them. Go figure.

So if you are going to dance with the liquid devil, you should at least take every precaution. The more safety stuff you have on board your kayak, the safer you will be. Period. You cannot avoid accidents and bad fortune, but you can be ready when the two-headed beast rears its ugly faces. Whether you're paddling skinny waters or venturing into the deep blue, shit happens. Not being ready when it does is a terrible feeling.

I may be accused of worrying too much, but I'd hate to be accused of not worrying enough. I can only imagine how much it would suck to watch my kayak sink below the water while wishing that I hadn't left my radio in the jeep. On the other hand, if I had taken all rational precautions but still ended up helpless in the hands of the wild sea—well, so be it.

Melodramatic? Not at all. I've been a mile from the beach on a glass-calm night when the clouds rolled in, the wind pumped up, and the sea turned ugly. Then I was glad that I had worried, because I'd also packed my rain gear, charged the batteries on my VHF, and stowed my safety light in the pocket of my PFD. I've been on the water when the wind was blowing so hard, it almost ripped the paddle from my hands; when the rain was falling so hard, my boat was filling faster than my scuppers could drain; when the current was running so hard I couldn't paddle against it. I've been there when things got out of control and I had to struggle and pray my way back to the safety of terra firma. Don't worry too much about worrying too much.

Many people say that kayak anglers are crazy: braving big water to catch big fish from a little boat. But responsible 'yakers take all the possibilities of risk into consideration, recognize their abilities and limitations, and paddle carefully. That's not crazy.

When it comes to fishfinders, GPS, and VHF, the line between accessory and necessity may not be clear. When it comes to whistles, lights, and PFD, however, it is: Do not leave home without them. In fact, the US Coast Guard requires operators of "nonmotorized" watercraft to carry a Type I, II, III, or V PFD, a signal whistle, and either a battery-powered signal light or three day/night flares. And that's just the tip of the iceberg; a responsible 'yaker will carry all the required safety stuff and more.

USCG-Mandated Must-Haves

The Coast Guard is stringent when it comes to safety requirements for motorboats, but pretty lax when it comes to nonmotorized watercraft. There are requirements, but they are probably better suited to the casual paddler than the serious 'yak angler.

Basically, according to the USCG, a nonmotorized boat operator must have a PFD (which needn't be worn at all times), a signal light (but only if the operator will be out after dark), and a sound device (with no limitations as to quality or quantity). That's it.

Unbelievably, many kayak anglers don't carry even these required safety items.

The first, a personal flotation device, is the most important. The Coast Guard has strict guidelines for manufacturers when it comes to building PFDs. A USCG-approved life vest will have a large label declaring its size, the weight minimum, and the chest size range of the wearer. The label will describe the type of vessel for which the jacket is intended. There are also a bunch of warnings and exemptions, including this one: "Do not carry heavy objects—heavy objects impair flotation." Ya think?

Yet strict as the USCG may be when it comes to designing life vests, it's vague in prescribing what life vest must accompany a kayaker. It approves all models, from Type I to Type V. That means you could use an orange, foam U-style life vest and fall under the USCG's requirements—but miss completely the requirements of serious kayaking.

Kayak angling demands a life vest that is comfortable and functional. Even though the Coast Guard mandates only that you have a vest aboard, common sense requires you to wear it all the time. Early in my kayaking career, I was fishing a short distance from a rock jetty in 10 feet of water. The day was calm, and I was only a short swim from shore. Regardless, I had my PFD on and latched. Out of nowhere, a thunderstorm brewed up. The wind started to howl, and I turned around in my boat to get my rain gear. Next thing I knew, I was in the water.

What happened?

What happened was I had turned my body downwind, raising the upwind gunnel of my kayak. This allowed the wind to get underneath my boat and flip me like a pancake. What if I had been reaching for my PFD instead of my rain gear? Worry about the what-ifs before they happen.

One thing I hear inexperienced kayakers (those who have yet to have "The Fear" scared into them) do is rationalize reckless behavior. "Oh, I'll just grab my PFD if it looks nasty." Or "I'm only fishing in knee-deep water. If I fall out, I'll just stand up." Then these guys get knocked out of the boat unexpectedly or happen to fall out in the middle of a deep channel and their carelessness becomes evident too late.

LIGHT

One of the more common ways for nonmotorized vessels to meet danger is when they meet with motorized vessels. Powerboaters are the archnemesis of paddle boaters. Don't get me wrong—it's not the boaters, it's the boats. I love to fish from a motorboat—and much prefer to zoom across the water under the power of twin 250 four-strokes than plod along under the power of my twin macaroni-noodle arms—so I understand all too well that a powerboat is powerful vehicle on which things happen fast and reactions can be slow.

The fact is that most powerboaters are not looking for kayakers, so kayakers must always be looking for their gas-powered siblings. I'm always listening for the drone of outboards on the water and always watching boaters when they're in the area. When kayak fishing at night, the visibility situation becomes critical.

Kayaks are practically invisible after dark. Low to the water and silent, a kayak will disappear when the sun goes down. I'd actually recommend you not fish in a kayak after dark . . . if the fishing weren't so good after dark. Fact is, some of the best angling opportunities are available between sunset and sunrise, so kayaking at night is unavoidable. Your best bet is to carry several lights and wear plenty of reflective material.

The most essential light is a battery-operated white navigation light. Several companies make these lamps, but the best are produced by manufacturers that specialize in paddle sports. Most are weak incandescent bulbs powered by heavy D batteries. These lamps tend to last about as long as the batteries that power them. After their first encounter with salt water, they're dead. Safety lights, like those made by Scotty Plastics, run for hours on two AA batteries and are so tough that you can permanently install them on your boat. Even

though the Coast Guard requires a light only at night, always have
one with you in case of fog or a longer-than-expected outing.

In order to see, and be seen, a paddler should also carry a LED
headlamp. These long-lasting, far-seeing lamps will shine light wherever you turn your head and also shine light into the eyes of any
oncoming boaters. In case of a serious emergency, nothing gets attention like a battery-operated strobe light. I carry a small high-powered
beacon in the pocket of my life vest and check the batteries every
few months to make sure the unit is ready when needed.

Whistle

A kayak is nearly silent as it glides over the water. Boaters not only
can't see it, but can't hear it, either. Many times I have paddled up on
boaters who are drifting or at anchor and totally unaware of my presence. I'll shout: "How's it goin'!" and the unsuspecting boaters will
jump out of their skin. That's how kayakers have fun.

Most boaters don't expect to see, let alone hear, kayakers. Sound
carries a long way over the water. While I'm fishing, I often hear guys
on boats talking as they speed by. Usually, one guy will yell to the other
over the screaming engines, "Look at the crazy guy in the kayak!"
Still, although you can hear them, boaters cannot hear the gentle
plunk of a kayak paddle passing through the water over the sound of
their roaring outboards. But they can hear a whistle.

I carry a "pea-less" boating whistle in the pocket of my life vest.
"Pea-less" means that the whistle doesn't use a BB, like a coach's
whistle, so it will not corrode or seize up. A good safety whistle has
a range of up to 3 miles. I use a tether to attach the bright yellow
whistle to a D-ring on my PFD; if I fall out, I can still make noise.

According to the Coast Guard's safe boating guide, there are several common sound signals used by watercraft operators. One blast
means that the boater intends to pass on the port (left) side. Two
blasts: starboard side. I remember this because *starboard* has two sylla-
bles—for two blasts. Three blasts means that the boat is backing up.
In the fog or black of night, one prolonged blast means that the boat
is under way, while a long blast followed by two short ones means a

sailboat is coming. Five short blasts of the whistle in rapid succession means the vessel's operator doesn't agree with or cannot understand another operator's intentions. This sound signal may also be accompanied by certain universally understood hand gestures.

Other Critical Equipment

Even though the USCG only requires 'yakers to have a PFD, carry a whistle, and use a light at night, common sense demands much more.

To be as safe as possible and ready for almost anything, a kayak angler should also have a VHF radio, compass, first-aid kit, patch kit, dewatering device, rope, knife, scissors, water, and food. Don't worry, carrying all this stuff won't sink the kayak—in fact, it may help keep it afloat in an emergency.

Actually, most of this equipment can be stuffed in a medium-sized dry bag and stored in the forward hatch of the kayak. The rest of these safety items can be used for other purposes and kept on hand for an emergency.

Navigation

Obviously, a compass is one of the most essential safety items on any boat. When you're paddling across large bodies of open water, the compass will keep you on course against the forces of current and wind. Navigating backwater creeks and guts, a compass will keep you heading in the right direction. I hate to even mention the dreaded fog. Pea soup can roll in with out warning, blinding and distorting a boater instantly. I know several anglers who have found themselves so deep in the fog that they couldn't find the beach—which was less than a mile away. A compass takes up little space and will take less than 15 minutes to install. Go with a small, marine compass that uses thick oil to control the roll of the dial. Even though a handheld hiking compass will work in a pinch, it may not offer the accuracy you need to stay on course in rough conditions.

Of course, a compass is good, but a GPS is better. With a GPS you know not only the direction you're traveling but also your location, distance from home, speed, and course. Still, even with a GPS, you should have a compass. First, the GPS functions best in concert with the compass: Use the GPS to find the course to a waypoint, then use the compass to stay on course. Second, a GPS will tell you what direction the kayak is moving, while a compass shows what direction the bow is pointing. Depending on current and wind, these two may be quite different—you must often paddle at an angle into current and tide to maintain course. I also use my compass to tell me what direction the wind is blowing, which can affect both fishing and paddling. I turn my kayak until I'm facing into the wind (I hear it howling equally in both ears), then look at the compass. While every angler doesn't need a GPS, every kayaker must have a compass.

COMMUNICATION

A cell phone is also an invaluable tool for kayak safety. A quick call to 911 will alert the authorities to send in the cavalry. However, anyone who has a cell phone knows they never seem to work when they're needed the most. And that's on dry land. Add water, and a cell phone becomes practically useless. Get a high-quality dry bag and keep the cell phone tucked away for emergencies, but don't expect to rely on it in a pinch. A VHF radio is more reliable and more appropriate on the water. As I've noted previously, a VHF can alert the Coast Guard of an emergency, and it also broadcasts National Oceanic and Atmospheric Administration Weather Service reports— a constant stream of information about weather and water conditions. In many instances, that alone will keep you out of trouble.

NOAA forecasts help you plan your kayak trips as well as monitoring conditions while you're out on the water. The forecast can change as quickly as the weather, and the buoy and weather station reports on NOAA radio give real-time information. Even if it's calm where you're padding, all hell could be breaking loose a few miles away. It pays to be familiar with the area where you're paddling so you understand where the weather stations are located and can track storms and fronts as they approach.

Of course, there is no better source for weather information than the kayaker's own intuition. More than once I've fought against a gusty blow while listening to a buoy a few miles away report calm conditions. I've also fished in a downpour while listening to the weather radio forecast sunny skies. On the other hand, I've also fished beautiful days that were forecast to be blowouts. Truth is, a weather resource is only as accurate as the information it receives from its sources—and even then a forecast is at best an educated guess. Nothing can trump the power of observation combined with common sense.

Regardless of the forecast and current conditions, eye the sky and the water and make your own decisions about the weather. Then watch what's happening in the sky and on the water, and stay aware of changes. Kayakers—who are close to the water, open to the wind, at the whim and will of each—become acutely in tune with both. Paddlers can often feel the weather deteriorating before it even deteriorates.

One night, in late fall, my buddy and I were fishing under the Chesapeake Bay Bridge Tunnel, blasting school-sized striper on almost every cast. The bay was so calm that I could see the reflection of the bridge, illuminated by the streetlights, in the mirror-flat water. The calm was interrupted only by the roaring tractor-trailers passing overhead and the *pop, twop, pop* of stripers sucking silversides off the surface. Distracted by the fish and lulled by the quiet, my buddy and I had fished our way a mile offshore.

When I stopped to look at the night sky, it seemed darker than usual. The darkness seemed closer, lower, like it was pressing down in the west. I called my buddy on the VHF: "Does it look like rain coming?"

He replied, "I can still see the towers at Langley." I squinted into the horizon and picked out the familiar landmarks to the west.

Still, I was bothered by the sky, and a little while later I looked up again to notice that the stars were definitely blocked out by thick clouds moving down the bay. I hit the call button again. "Looks like we got some weather moving in."

My buddy came back, "I'm not quitting for anything. I listened to the report before I left the house."

We returned to the fish that were busting all around us, inhaling anything that hit the water. Then I felt a light puff of wind. It felt wrong. I picked up my radio and told my buddy, "I'm outta here!"

This time he came back, "I'm right behind you."

It was a long paddle back to the beach, across icy-cold water, and the clouds were definitely closing in from the west. When I caught up with my fishing buddy, we stopped to batten down the hatches and squeeze into our neoprene pullovers. The line of dark clouds was almost on us when we dug in to haul ass for the beach. At one point I looked up to see the starry sky cut perfectly in half by heavy clouds—the storm was coming straight for us.

As the front passed directly overhead, I got on the VHF and announced, "Here it comes!" Then things got real ugly. The wind kicked up to 20 knots and the sea jumped into a frothy mess. Our only saving grace was that the wind was coming in from the northwest, which is a death knell on the Chesapeake Bay . . . unless you're paddling southeast in a kayak. We used the tailwind and the following sea to our advantage, surfing back to shore across half a mile of roiling chop. The waves were breaking waist-high when we hit the beach. My kayak did a half roll, dumping me in the knee-deep water a few yards from shore. Ungraceful dismount aside, I was happy to be back on dry ground. I turned to see the bay's waves slapping and punching—an angry adversary that I had ducked once again. Whew.

When calamity strikes on the open water, a kayak angler's best safety resource is other kayak anglers, and a VHF radio is the best way to keep in touch. Although kayak anglers should avoid fishing alone, fishing within shouting distance—even visual contact—can be tough because one angler inevitably zigs while the other will zag. More than once I've turned around and found myself completely alone even though I'd left the launch with half a dozen other guys. A quick shout on the radio assures me that my companions are still afloat and ready to assist if I should need help.

Still, the fact of the matter is that kayak anglers can't really offer much help to peers who find themselves in trouble. Besides providing moral support, there is little one kayaker can do for another in distress. Depending on the size of the kayak and the size of the kayaker, it may be possible to double up on one boat and paddle a stranded 'yaker back to safety. Honestly, though, rescue is difficult without putting yourself in danger. One kayaker in the kayak and one in the water is better than two kayakers in the water. So the VHF is an essential safety item that can be used to call in help for yourself or a buddy who is hopelessly floundering in the sea.

BLADES

Many safety items have thousands of "peacetime" uses. For example, I always carry a towrope long enough to attach to another kayak that is dead in the water, throw to a floating buddy, or tie to a buoy or piling to keep from being swept away. I make sure my rope is available if I should need it in a pinch.

A knife and a pair of scissors can also get a kayak out of trouble quickly. One night I was negotiating a tricky inlet, using every ounce of strength and determination to paddle against the current and through a series of dangerous rips. I was terrified, on the edge of catastrophe, focusing hard at the shoreline ahead and hoping I would reach it. I had just convinced myself that I was going to make it when a bucktail followed by an arch of braided line flew over the bow of my kayak.

"What the . . . !" I yelled. Someone on the beach had cast his line across my boat. I was paddling so furiously that I quickly found myself tangled in virtually unbreakable braided line. With every stroke the tangle got worse, wrapping around my paddle and tying me up in knots. I couldn't stop paddling to untangle the line or the current would have swept me into the raging rips and bridge pilings. I reached for my scissors and realized that I had left them in the jeep.

That's when I learned to always carry a knife and a pair of scissors on my kayak. Somehow I managed to paddle to the beach and untangle the line of the very apologetic surf fisherman. He was lucky: I was too glad to be alive to worry about killing him.

There are all kinds of opportunities for a kayaker to become entangled in lines. Anchor ropes, paddle leashes, fishing rigs, monofilament, braided line, crab pot buoys, or nets could each ruin a kayak fishing trip. There are also many opportunities for a kayak angler to use scissors and a knife while fishing.

In an emergency, I'll usually reach for my scissors before my knife. Scissors are safer than an open blade, offering less chance to slice yourself inadvertently as you cut yourself out of a mess. Of course some materials, like rope or leash, require a sharper blade, so I always carry a knife on my life vest.

The knife should be light, small, flat, very sharp, and easy to attach to any part of your life vest. Only use it when you need it in an emergency—not when you need it to cut bait. Keep the knife sharp, oiled, and clipped to an out-of-the-way yet easy-to-reach place on your PFD. Several companies make a safety knife that features a plastic hook with a sharp blade in the bend. This type of knife stows easily on a strap or in a pocket and allows you to cut rope without cutting yourself.

Being held underwater by tangled ropes is the worst nightmare of any water sport enthusiast. That nightmare came true for a good buddy of mine on Virginia's Eastern Shore one spring day. We were drum fishing the shoals that stretch across Fishermans Island inlet when my friend hooked into a huge redfish. The bull pulled him into the waves that were crashing on the shallow shoals, and his kayak flipped. At that point he became hopelessly entangled in his paddle leash, held underwater, unable to escape from beneath the boat, desperate. Luckily the leash was old, and the webbing had rotted to the point that he was able to break it and swim free. But what if it had been new? Now he carries a knife on his life vest, and so do I.

PUMPS

Even though a sit-on-top kayak doesn't risk filling with water the way a sit-in kayak does, the possibility exists that the boat can take on water, fill, flip, and sink. Whereas any SINK paddler would be ready to bail the boat, most SOT anglers are unprepared for water in the hold. I sure wasn't ready to bail when my boat developed a small hole and filled with water one night. I was a mile offshore in sloppy conditions when I noticed that something about my kayak didn't feel right. The boat was hard to turn and difficult to keep upright. I could hear something banging inside it. Since it was too rough to open the hatch, I worked my way toward shore. Once I reached calmer water, I slid forward and opened my bow hatch to look inside. Much to my shock, the boat was filled almost to the rim with water—gallons and gallons of water—and my extra paddle was floating around the hold. I stroked frantically for the beach, just making it to safety before my 'yak disappeared under the dark waves.

After I reached shore, I recovered the kayak, flipped it, and inspected it for damage. There was a hole in the keel about the size of a pencil tip—wide enough to let in gallons of water over a couple of hours. After years of dragging the kayak from the car to the water, I had worn right through the plastic in the bottom of the boat.

The scariest thing about the incident is that I didn't even realize my boat was full of water until I looked in the hatch. Even though it was behaving strangely, I never thought it was about to sink. In fact, had the boat filled further, it would have become impossible to control and eventually rolled over, dumping me in the water and leaving me stranded. It still amazes me that I was able to make it back to the beach with a hull two-thirds filled with water. My Prowler stayed afloat and upright long after it should have flipped and gone to the bottom.

What if I'd been farther offshore, or the water had been coming in faster? I didn't even have a cup to bail with. Now I carry an emergency kit put together by Scotty Plastics that includes a towrope, extra flashlight, and whistle, all stored in a watertight canister that's the perfect size for bailing. I also carry a tube of Marine Goop silicone to patch small holes. Even better, Scotty makes several hand pumps that will empty water faster than it can run in. For the ultimate in safety, strap one of these bad boys to your milk crate and have it ready for the worst-case scenario.

First Aid

Of course the worst-case scenario for any kayak angler would involve an injury. Since a kayak's engine is you, any cut, scrape, pull, or fracture is equivalent to a breakdown. Fortunately, kayaking is a low-impact sport, and kayakers don't usually encounter injuries the way skateboarders, mountain bikers, or rock climbers do. But fishing involves sharp objects, and those sharp objects occasionally find their way into your soft skin. No angler should be caught on the water without a simple first-aid kid. Scotty Plastics also makes a kayak-friendly kit that's conveniently housed in a watertight container and includes 85 lifesaving items, but a basic kit should at least include Band-Aids, medical tape, antiseptic cream or wipes, half a dozen ibuprofen tablets, and a space blanket. The space blanket is among the most essential items, since hypothermia is one of the most dangerous threats you'll face.

The other common danger is getting hooked. For this reason, I avoid using treble hooks from the kayak at all costs. Especially since most of the fish I land end up in my lap. That's no place to have a berserk fish shaking a bunch of sharp hooks.

A hook lodged in your hand will make it difficult to paddle and might make it impossible to return to the beach. Most of the time the hook can be removed on site. If the point hasn't passed through your skin, double a 24-inch section of 50-pound mono around the hook bend. Push the eye flat against your skin, and yank the line to pull the hook out. The idea is to allow the barb to exit the skin without causing more damage. If that doesn't work, or if the hook is sticking through an exit wound, simply clip off the point and barb with a pair of dikes and back the hook out. Of course these procedures are easier said than done, but being prepared to perform on-the-water surgery can mean the difference between having to be rescued and returning to the dock under your own power.

KICKER PADDLE

For a kayaker, losing a paddle is like losing an engine. Paddles can break, bend, split, or just float away. An extra set of blades—even just a cheap eggbeater—can save the day should you become separated from your paddle. I keep an extra paddle in the hold of my kayak. The two-piece paddle is broken down, lashed together, and tied to my transducer so that I can access it in an emergency. Like a PFD, an extra paddle is one of those safety items that give you peace of mind on the water. As long as I have a backup power source, I feel confident to go farther, stay out longer, and fish harder.

FOOD AND WATER

The absolute worst-case scenario (short of burial at sea) would find you unable to get home on your own. Even though I've never had to be rescued, the potential is out there every time I paddle away from the beach. So prepare for the worst. In case of an unexpected extended stay on the water, always pack at least a couple of energy bars and an extra bottle of water.

It is surprising how hungry you can get on the water. If you're the kayak's engine, then food is your fuel. Paddling hard through adverse conditions will quickly run your tank empty. There may be no gas left for fishing! I always take along a couple Clif Bars to keep my mind on the fish and off my stomach. On a long trip, running out of grub could be dangerous, leaving your calorie reserve spent while you're still a long way from the next gas station. Water is even more important. Dehydration can lead to fatigue, heatstroke, even loss of consciousness. A kayaker should drink at least a quart of water every hour—especially in the heat. Be sure to drink and eat, even if you're not thirsty or hungry.

CLOTHES

Also pack some extra clothes in case the weather changes unexpectedly. I once read about a kayaker in New York City who got an itch to go for a short paddle after work. Lightly dressed and with no provisions, he dropped in to his kayak club, grabbed a boat, and went for what he thought would be a short paddle around the harbor. Once on the water, and a mile away from the shore, a thick bank of fog moved in, isolating the guy from both banks of the river and leaving him blindly paddling close to the shipping lanes. Eventually he found himself in a marsh, where he had to spend the night in shorts and a T-shirt until the sun rose and burned off the fog. In the middle of one of the world's biggest cities, surrounded by 18 million people, this kayaker was completely alone—helpless.

After reading this tale, I always pack at least a rain jacket and often a pair of rain pants. These packable items take up little room—in fact, they fit perfectly in the pouch behind my Surf to Summit Elite seat—and offer peace of mind when I'm on the water. Even in midsummer, rain and wind can send you into hypothermia. Regardless of the time of year, type of kayaking trip, or experience level, you can't be too careful.

Acceptable Risk

Jim Sammons, a well-known, California-based kayak fishing guide, has a poignant story posted on his Web site (www.kayak4fish.com) to illustrate the complexity of kayak safety. In the story, a kayak guide took three tourists off the coast of California to watch whales. Once the group had paddled offshore, strong Santa Ana winds came up from the east, pushing the kayakers farther out to sea. With little experience or conditioning, the tourists quickly became fatigued and were unable to paddle back to the launch. The guide was able to tow one of his charges to safety but abandoned the other two paddlers. One of these two victims fell into the water and became separated from her boat. She spent two hours in 60-degree water clinging to a lobster pot buoy before the Coast Guard helicopter could rescue her. The second kayaker was 7 miles out when the Coast Guard cutter came by.

Like most kayak horror stories, this one started out innocently enough. The guide had the best intentions, and his clients had the highest confidence in him. No one intentionally took careless risks. Had things gone well, and the wind not blown, everything would have been fine. But things didn't go well, and the wind did blow, and everything was not fine.

Stories like this teach several valuable lessons that are also covered on Sammons's site.

First, experienced paddlers are responsible for the fate of newbies. More than once, I've taken rookie anglers along on hairy trips, only to find my companions in over their heads. Sure, it's hard to tell folks, "Sorry, you're not good enough to go on this trip." But it's more difficult to save them from drowning or tow them back when they become exhausted. I usually explain the requirements of a trip, the dangers and challenges involved, and the potential consequences should things go wrong. Then I leave it to the anglers to judge their capacity for the undertaking on their own.

Second, never paddle out farther than you can paddle in if the weather turns bad. With a tailwind and a following current, it's surprising how far you can paddle. With a headwind and opposing current, it's equally surprising how difficult paddling can be. Plus, if you've already covered some distance on the way out, you may have no energy left to fight the elements on the way in. It's a good idea to know how far you can paddle. Take a day trip and cover some distance to determine your range. My personal limit is 15 miles round trip. Yes, I've paddled farther, and I could probably double that if I had to, but I'm confident that I could cover 15 miles in almost any conditions, so that's where I set my boundary.

Third, whenever possible you should start your trip paddling *into* the wind and current. These two forces can be your greatest enemy or best friend. With some careful planning, you can stack the cards in your favor. When organizing long trips for big fish, I always plan the paddle out to the fishing grounds and the trek back to the launch to coincide with prevailing currents and winds—paddling out on the ebb, say, and returning on the flood. Of course, current can only be predicted to a certain extent—tides don't always follow the tide chart, and the wind doesn't always follow the forecast—but if you can get at least one of the two in your favor, life will be that much easier.

Fourth, as Sammons tells anglers, "Dress to swim and rig to flip." Expect to end up in the water every time you get in your kayak even if you've never fallen out before. Wear clothes that will allow you to stay warm even when wet. Keep lines, hooks, blades, and other dangerous things stored so that they don't tangle or cut you when you fall out of your 'yak or crawl back in. Lash everything of value to the kayak; if it isn't tied down, it's sure to end up in the drink. If you go over, your priority should be to hold on to the paddle. It is easier to swim to the kayak while dragging the paddle than swim to the paddle while dragging the kayak. And of course, always wear your PFD.

Fifth, practice makes perfect. The best way to prepare for disaster is to practice it. Take your kayak out on a relatively calm day in a controlled environment and practice flipping and reentering your boat. Rock the boat side-to-side to test its stability. Go through surf launches and landings. Take a paddling course with a certified instructor. The more experience you have in the water, the more confident you'll feel on the water. When conditions get ugly, I'll constantly remind myself that I've been through worse and survived several dunkings. This helps me stay calm and focus on getting back to the launch. Be sure to train with a partner so that "practice" doesn't turn into the real thing. And of course, wear your PFD.

Depending on the kayak or the kayaker, reentering the boat from the water could be very difficult. Big guys will have a hard time getting back in a little boat. In general, sit-on-top kayaks are easier to reenter than their sit-in counterparts—another reason for the SOT's popularity with anglers. Paddlers who choose to use a SINK must enroll in a kayak safety course to learn how to get back in the boat if they fall out.

SOT paddlers would also benefit from a safety course, but reentry can be broken down into three steps: *Belly, Butt, Feet*.

From the water, swim up to the side of the kayak. Be sure to keep the kayak down wind, down tide, or on the down side of the surf. Reach across the boat with both hands, grab the far handle, and pull yourself belly-down across the cockpit. From there, roll over and slide your butt into the seat, then swing your feet over the side and into the foot wells. Voilà, back in the saddle.

Although remounting the kayak after an unplanned dismount may be intimidating for some anglers, don't underestimate the power of adrenaline. The few times I've ended up in the water, I was back in my boat before I even got wet. However, I know other anglers who have fallen into the water and were unable to reenter their boats. Even with the best training, there are no guarantees of safety. Always have a backup plan and a backup plan for your backup plan.

Safety Is Your Choice

Although every possible scenario cannot possibly be anticipated, responsible kayakers lose a lot of sleep worrying about what-ifs. *What if the wind comes up? What if it rains? What if I get hurt? What if the current is too strong? What if my boat develops a hole? What if I lose my paddle? What if I end up in the water?* You can't expect the unexpected, but you should at least expect the expectable.

Sure, over hundreds of hours of water time, I've never needed any of the safety stuff. But I carry it every time I leave the dock. That's good. I've never used my safety beacon, channel 16 on my VHF, my extra paddle, or even my PFD. Still, my philosophy is that it's better to have this stuff and not need it than to need it and not have it!

The image that keeps me up at night is needing a safety item and realizing I left it in the car or failed to bring it at all. Treading water while watching my kayak sink and wishing I had my PFD. Watching my paddle drift away in the current and remembering that the backup is in my car. Having to return to the beach due to hunger pangs that could have been satiated with an energy bar. Getting tied up in my paddle leash and held underwater, struggling and holding my breath, reaching for my emergency knife . . . that isn't there. Watching a boat barrel down on me and having no whistle to alert the driver of my presence. Paddling hopelessly in the fog without a compass. Slipping into hypothermia because I didn't bring a jacket or space blanket. With an active imagination, a kayak angler can picture a horror film full of nightmare scenarios—yet some accidents remain unimaginable.

One afternoon I was standing in my 'yak drifting down a little creek while sight casting to red drum. As I moved with the current, I noticed some huge mullet—up to 5 pounds—scurrying away. When I reached a bend in the creek, I saw the water in front of me boiling with fish. A deep hole had formed where the banks of the creek made a sharp bend, and it was full of giant mullet. As I drifted closer, one of the mullet (a good 6-pounder) jumped upstream trying to escape. Then another leaped over the bow of my kayak to safety. That's when I realized that things were going to get really bad. I didn't want to sit down because I didn't want to take one of these fish to the head. Just as I considered another tender target in need of protection, a mullet missile hit me dead in the crotch. Now I was doubled over in pain, with a huge mullet thrashing in the cockpit of my boat and my balance giving way. I fell into the cauldron of writhing mullet, fish pummeling me from all directions. Luckily I had my life vest on to take the brunt of the attack and was able to scramble up the slippery, muddy bank to safety. Goes to prove, you never know what is going to happen when you push off terra firma and head out into the wild blue. You gotta be prepared for any-thing—I mean *anything*.

4

Modifying the Kayak

Kayak anglers look at their craft as a canvas and the spectrum of kayak fishing accessories as their palette of paint. Putting together an effective, efficient, ergonomic fishing platform is like creating a work of art that reflects your own style, personality, and needs. From a hastily slapped together plastic jalopy to a carefully crafted custom rig, the range of kayak systems is as varied as the range of kayak anglers.

Tools of the Trade
Even for the mechanically inept, rigging and outfitting a kayak is relatively simple. The kayak craftsman will need only a handful of tools, most of which can be found in the garage or kitchen gadget drawer, and some basic skills. A couple of specialty tools will be required, but these are readily available at any big-box store or home improvement center.

First, you want to assemble a collection of hardware. Many accessory kits don't include the hardware for installation, so it's a good idea to stock up on stainless-steel Phillips-head screws and lock nuts in various lengths and widths. Of course, a Phillips-head screwdriver makes driving Phillips-head screws easier—but investing in a rechargeable power driver makes installation super-easy.

Since kayak anglers always seem to be drilling holes in their boats, a high-quality drill will be your best friend. Remember the adage *Measure twice and drill once* when deciding where to pierce your boat. Holes are easy to make and hard to fill. To carve PVC pipe and other plastics, use a jigsaw.

To attach seats, leashes, lines, and crates, use eye loops and zip ties. These two fasteners have a million uses on a kayak, so be sure to have half a million of each on hand at all times. In fact, I carry half a dozen zip ties of various lengths and widths in my crate in case I need to cinch something up or tie it down while on the water.

Bungee cords and parachute cords also come in handy on the water. Keep a selection of each in stock both at home and on the boat. From fixing broken handles to tying down rods, tackle, and gear, bungee cords and rope are indispensable tools of the trade.

Most of this stuff can be found lying around the house. However, a kayak customizer will need a couple of special tools that will be called on again and again.

First, to attach accessories to areas of the kayak where you can't access the bottom of the deck, you'll want a rivet gun. This simple tool allows you to secure an accessory tightly to the deck and reduce the risk of it pulling free.

Before deciding to use a rivet to install an accessory, of course, make sure the rivet will fit through the hole in that accessory and the head will have enough flat space to lie flat against the flange. To use the rivet gun, first drill a hole in the hull that is the exact diameter of the rivet. Put the accessory's hole over the rivet, and push the flat end of the rivet through both openings. Place the pointed end of the rivet in the nipple of the rivet gun and press against the hull. Squeeze the rivet gun's handle until the rivet comes tight on the inside of the kayak. Keep tightening the rivet until the rivet gun snaps its shaft flush with its head.

To remove an improperly installed rivet, drill out the center with a bit just smaller than its shaft. Also, a misplaced drill hole in the hull can be plugged with a rivet until it can be properly repaired. Not only will there be plenty of opportunities to use a rivet gun on your own boat, but your buddies will forever be coming over to use it on theirs.

Another handy tool is a 2½-inch hole saw to drill the opening for a flush-mounted rod holder. The hole saw will pay for itself by drilling perfectly round, perfectly sized holes for the rod holder. Do not attempt this installation with a handsaw.

With a handful of simple tools and a pocket full of fasteners, you're armed and ready to go to work customizing your kayak.

Starting in the Stern

Starting from the back of the boat and moving forward, the first item to consider is the stern handle. This is one of the most used appendages on the kayak. You'll spend a great deal of time dragging the boat from the car to the beach to the launch to the car to the garage to the yard, so a well-placed, ergonomic, indestructible handle is indispensable.

Most kayaks have a handle in the stern. But not all handles are effectively installed or conveniently positioned. If the rear handle isn't comfortable or well placed, you can move it or install another handle.

Several companies make easy-grip handles for kayaks, but a wooden dowel with a hole drilled through it will work in a pinch. To install the handle, get an eye loop and two rivets. Find a flat section in the stern on the centerline. Be sure to consider carefully the placement of this loop before drilling holes. Will the kayak be balanced starboard-to-port? Will the angle of the handle allow you to drag the boat comfortably? Will the handle interfere with other things on the boat, such as a rudder or the paddle cradle? Is the plastic thick enough to support the full weight of the boat? Will the rivet pass through something on the other side of the plastic? Be sure to look at the prospective handle placement from every angle and think through every possibility before making any holes.

Once you've picked out a good spot, attach the loop with two rivets. Install the handle according to the manufacturer's instructions, being sure that all knots or connections are strong and secure. Nothing is funnier than watching someone who's dragging a kayak have the handle comes loose, sending him flat on his ass. Hilarious, unless it's you.

Rudder

One of the most common questions kayak anglers ask when rigging is, "Do I need a rudder?" There are two answers to that question: yes and no.

Yes, a rudder makes life easier. When paddling with a rudder, you can turn the boat on a dime. On a long trip, you can set the rudder at an angle that compensates for the forces of wind and current, making it easier to paddle straight toward your destination. With a rudder, you can maintain your cadence over a long distance, saving paddle strokes and traveling farther with less effort. Not only that, but when you're fishing you can use the rudder to hold the boat in the current; that lets you work an area longer without needing the paddle to adjust your position. Remember, it's hard to paddle and fish at the same time. So, yes, life is easier with a rudder. But do you need one?

No—you don't *need* a rudder, and, in some instances you may not want one. I can't count the number of times that I've had to untangle a buddy's line from his rudder. What would he have done if he'd been fishing alone? A tangled rudder could easily cause you to become immobilized, flip over, or at least end the day's fishing. With all the wires, rigging, blades, and pedals on a kayak, in certain circumstances a rudder can actually become a liability. Anglers who fish tight to structure such as bridge pilings or jetties, as well as those who launch through the surf, are asking for trouble with a rudder. Such pursuits will eventually cause the rudder to break or even separate from the boat. With so many moving parts and open holes in the boat, a broken rudder could cost a fishing trip or more.

So do you need a rudder? The answer is: yes *and* no. With or without it, you can't go wrong. The disadvantages of having a rudder pretty much cancel out the advantages, leaving the choice up to you.

Tank Well: The Kayak Trunk

The tank well is arguably a fishing kayak's most significant feature. After all, the large, open space behind the seat is really what a makes a kayak a fishing kayak. So, as a fisherman, be sure that the well is large enough to carry all the stuff that you can't leave home without. Thankfully most kayak companies are designing boats to maximize storage space. Designers like Allen Stancil at Liquidlogic are extending the tank well from gunnel to gunnel and all the way back to the stern handle.

At the least, the tank well should be large enough to accommodate an office crate—arguably the second most important feature on a fishing kayak. The office crate (milk crate) has become ubiquitous with fishing kayaks. In fact, several companies have even designed kayak-specific crates and accessories that are designed to be used with these plastic catchalls.

The kayak crate is another area where you can let your creativity shine. With a webwork of plastic supports, there are a million places to tie, clip, snap, and screw on accessories. The crate can hold everything from rod holders, to a cooler, a light, a stringer, leashes, a tether, even a live well. I throw my drink bottles in there and hang lures on the crossbars to dry. Extra lengths of rope get jammed into the cracks; my anchor is wedged in the back.

The true genius of my crate setup revolves around a hard-sided, soft cooler that I found at a local sporting goods store. The cooler, made by California Innovations, fits perfectly in my crate, tight enough side-to-side to stay put when I flip my boat while at the same time allowing enough space front and back for me to install rod holders, stick my lip gripper, and carry my landing net.

Once again, realizing the profit potential in kayak fishing, companies are rushing to the rescue of kayak anglers with purpose-built crate caddies. Products like the Crate Mate by 3rd Grip are designed specifically for kayak anglers. This fade-resistant, rip-proof-denier crate system keeps all the stuff you can stuff into a 13-by-13 office crate dry and secure. The Crate Mate can be closed with Velcro tabs and plastic snaps to keep lunch, loose lures, bags of jig tails, a head-lamp, and suntan lotion dry and secure.

This crate system also includes a shoulder strap, making it a great way to carry gear from the house to the car and the car to the kayak. When you're making a long-distance launch, it's best to drag the empty kayak to the water, then return for the paddle, rods, elec-tronics, and crate full of tackle and accessories.

I stick my cell phone, money, and fishing license, along with extra batteries, binoculars, camera, and a couple of emergency energy bars, in a dry bag and stuff it inside the "trunk." The Crate Mate also has large pockets on the outside that accommodate tackle trays and bags of soft plastics. This way I'm not constantly accessing the inside of the box to get my hands on the lures, hooks, and terminal tackle I use the most. The outside compartments also give me a place to hold wet stuff. A functional tank well is the key to a functional kayak fisherman.

Even in the absence of this particular storage option, most anglers can find some way to keep their stuff dry and secure. Dry bags are a great option, allowing you to use several bags to store dif-ferent stuff: one for personal effects, one for soft baits; one for hard baits, another for leader material. Hard cases such as OtterBoxes, which are sealed against water and nearly indestructible, will hold sharp stuff like plugs and lures or crushable items like a cell phone or camera. Not only are these bags and boxes impervious to water, but they float so you have a better chance to recover your gear in the event of a "wet exit." Fold the mouth of the bag over three times, snap the gasket closed, and use a carabiner to clip the bag to one of the plastic supports onto the crate. Dry boxes can be clipped to the kayak crate as well. Be sure to choose boxes and bags that are clear so you can see their contents without having to open the bag and dig around to find something.

It's a good idea to keep a laminated card with your name, address, and phone number in each bag in case it's lost and later recovered by someone else. One of my buddies deep-sixed his dry bag with car keys, camera, cell phone, money, credit cards, and ID in the surf off Fishermans Island on the north side of the Chesapeake Bay. Two weeks later the bag was found by a beachcomber 15 miles away at Cape Henry on the south side of the bay's mouth. It's a big ocean, but it can be a small world.

In addition to dry storage, the kayak crate holds a variety of other essentials. The webwork of plastic supports offer limitless opportunities to attach vertical rod holders with zip ties. Simple holders can be made out a piece of 2-inch PVC tubing; for rods with larger butts, use 2½-inch tubing. To carry fly rods upright, use a jigsaw to cut a 1-inch-wide slit down two-thirds of the PVC pipe to accommodate the reel seat. Anglers fishing in heavy cover may want to install PVC rod holders at an angle on the side of the crate. Simply use zip ties to lash a length of pipe at a 45-degree angle on each side of the crate to provide more clearance while passing under low-hanging branches, bridges, or piers.

Another creative use for PVC comes from a good buddy of mine, Chris Lindstad, who is a chronic tinkerer. He took a 1-foot length of 2-inch PVC and warmed it with a heat gun. Then, using asbestos-lined gloves, he squeezed the malleable plastic into an oval that will hold his lip gripper. A shorter piece of molded PVC holds his pliers. Each is mounted on the outside of his crate at an angle that allows easy access yet keeps these items from falling overboard. Pretty cool.

The kayak crate also provides a variety of options for clipping leashes and bungees in order to tether expensive things to the boat. A general rule of thumb is, *Don't take anything on the kayak you don't want to lose.* Another is, *If you don't tie it down, you will lose it.* Just because you take expendable rods, reels, electronics, net, tackleboxes, and the like doesn't mean you want to lose them. To keep this stuff in the boat, keep this stuff tied down. I use two systems to attach my gear to my boat. While I'm under way, I have a bungee cord stretched across the soft-sided cooler, keeping my stuff in the cooler and the cooler in my boat. My rods are lined up along the crate; another bungee stretched across the reels keeps them in place. While I'm fishing, I use leashes by Surf to Summit to keep expensive rods in the boat. These leashes are attached to the rod with a Velcro cuff leading to a strong cord, which is connected to my milk crate with a brass clip. Surf to Summit leashes also have a plastic clip at the base of the Velcro cuff, making it possible to quickly detach the rod from the leash in an emergency.

A variation on the kayak crate. This stripped-down crate allows the angler to carry everything he needs and nothing he doesn't. Also, the crate keeps dry stuff out of the water while making a shelf for wet stuff beneath.

A prudent angler keeps everything in his boat tied down; a careless one does not. I always keep my lip gripper on a leash. The *one time* I neglected to attach it to the leash, I lost the lip gripper overboard. Really. I usually keep my rods tethered with Surf to Summit rod leashes in the vertical holders, and I always keep my VHF tethered to my PFD. While I'm fishing, I usually remove the leash from my rod, choosing to sacrifice my tackle before sacrificing conveniences. Obviously anglers using fancy, high-dollar equipment would want to sacrifice a little comfort for a lot of dough.

The crate and any closed storage system like Crate Mate or my cooler are also perfect places to stash tackleboxes and bags of grubs. However, constantly accessing the storage compartment or rummaging around for tackle is not convenient. Also, the crate on some 'yaks is too far back to reach without turning 180 degrees in the cockpit.

For example, my Ocean Kayak Prowler has a recessed cutout in the well, right behind the seat, that's a perfect fit for three tackle trays. In fact, the well was specifically designed to hold a Plano marine tacklebox that will accommodate two Plano tackle trays. This system keeps tackle dry and secured in the boat, but makes it difficult to access the boxes for quick lure changes. Again, a trade-off: safe, dry tackle for convenience.

I choose to keep my tackle in several "water-resistant" tackleboxes made by Plano. These boxes are perfect for kayak anglers: They incorporate a watertight seal and latches on three sides to keep most water out of the lure compartments. Still, on a kayak nothing is waterproof. These boxes will take on water when submerged, and opening and closing the box inevitably lets water in. I lose more tackle to corrosion than I do to snags, breakoffs, and big fish. After a particularly wet fishing trip, I open my boxes, spray off the lures and hooks with fresh water, and coat everything with WD-40. I hang wet lures on my crate, then spray them down when I spray my boat off. I keep complete boxes for each type of fishing I do. That way, whether I'm heading out for big game, big stripers, light tackle, or bottom fishing, I've only got to grab one box and I'm ready to go.

Kayak anglers are constantly worried about weight. Every extra ounce is an extra ounce you have to paddle around. For some boats and anglers, too much weight may make the craft unsafe. On the other hand, heading out to bottom fish, jig, or fish for big game inevitably involves loading the boat with heavy sinkers and lures. Then add lunch, water bottles, rods and reels, a couple of buckets of chum, and an anchor! Before you know it, the boat will barely be above the water.

I've seen guys pack everything *and* the kitchen sink to go fishing, then tire themselves out paddling all the extra weight around. Just because you can fit it in your kayak doesn't mean you can take it with you. The problem is, most anglers constantly worry, *If I don't take it, I'll need it.* On the other hand, if you do take it, you'd better be ready to lug it around all day. Before each trip, I carefully dig through my tackle, sorting my stuff into three categories: what I need, what I might need, and what I don't need. Then I cut out a third of what I need and half of what I might need. To control my own can't-leave-it-behind syndrome, I limit my tackle to what I can stuff into one of the aforementioned tackle trays. Tough decisions must be made in kayak fishing. If it won't fit in the tank well, it don't go on the trip.

Cockpit: Safe and Comfy

Moving out of the tank well and into the cockpit, we go from carrying gear to carrying the angler. Two considerations must be taken into account when laying out the kayak's cockpit: safety and comfort.

The first consideration, safety, is more important. Jim Sammons, the California big-water 'yak guide, stresses, "Rig to flip." The possibility of ending up in the water must be foremost on your mind as you design the layout of your boat. First, keep all sharp objects sheathed or stored in the crate to avoid inadvertently slicing yourself if the boat should go over. Keep all loose lines—including fishing lines, anchor line, mooring lines, and leashes—secured so you don't get tangled should you end up in the water. Try to keep loose pointy objects like lures and hooks from accumulating in the cockpit. To keep wet lures handy but out of the way, hang them on the crate behind you. Store leader material, rods you're not currently using, and leashes in the tank well. The idea is to keep the cockpit free of anything that might tangle you up if you flip.

Try to keep the cockpit clear and uncluttered, keep rod holders to a minimum, mount electronics flush to the deck, and avoid installing pegs, pads, or pedals in the foot wells. First, every object that sticks out of the cockpit will snare fishing lines, snag lures, and tangle the landing net when it is needed the most. So keep hardware mounted flush with the deck and accessories out of your lap. Second, a pile of crap in the cockpit makes it hard to get in and out of the boat—whether it's a planned or an unplanned exit. Always be mindful of your stuff. When you see a knife in the cockpit, put it away. When you see scissors lying in the foot well, put them away. When you see treble hooks, jigs, or rigs, your first thought should be, *That's gonna hurt.* Then put them away.

Okay, so I'm a minimalist who believes that an uncluttered boat is the sign of an uncluttered mind. Some guys prefer to take everything they own on the 'yak and leave it lying on the deck in plain sight. The problem with the omniscient approach to organizing tackle is that pieces will inevitably get lost, hooks will end up stuck in clothes or flesh—a frantic fish flopping in your lap will cause a tackle explosion. That's why I go for the a-place-for-everything-and-everything-in-its-place approach.

Other anglers like to keep electronics, rods, rigs, and tackle in easy reach, preferring to use rod-holder extenders and RAM Mounts to put all their bells and whistles at arm's length. The problem is that a lot of the action in a kayak takes place in the kayaker's lap. Lures are tied, reels are reeled, and fish are landed all on your knees. It's crucial to keep this area free of obstructions—a thrashing fish can cause a lot of chaos, damaging anything that gets in its way. Not only that, but some kayakers turn their boats into plastic coffins by mounting accessories, rod holders, and tackle systems in places that make it impossible to get out of or back into the boat in an emergency. As Sammons says, you gotta rig your boat to flip—take every worst-case scenario into account, then keep the cockpit free of obstructions and snags that could endanger you.

Of course, the kayak's cockpit should be not just safe, but comfortable, too. Consider that kayak fishing may require you to sit in one position for many hours with no real chance to stretch your legs. In fact, this can be one of the most difficult physical challenges you'll overcome. Forget the arms—kayaking is tough on the legs, hips, and butt.

Take a Seat

Each angler has to solve the comfort problem individually. Luckily, there are a lot of options and accessories to customize a cockpit into a floating Barcalounger. Even fishing kayaks that come off the assembly line with a factory-installed seat can be customized to maximize comfort and ergonomics. Factory seat are generally designed as one-size-fits-all units, yet kayak anglers come in many different sizes. If the standard seat is comfy—good for you. If not, install any one of the many aftermarket units available. These seats come in a variety of sizes, shapes, and forms, allowing you to pick the model that best fits your kayak and your kayaking.

These aftermarket seats offer more support and padding than most factory models and also allow you to remove the seat and transfer it to another boat—taking your Barcalounger with you. Most kayak seats have straps that attach to eye rings in front of the seat and behind it. In addition to offering limitless possibilities for adjustment, these straps also make the seat more stable, giving you solid support for hard paddling. When custom-installing a seat, be sure to place the eye rings where they won't get in the way of the paddle or the paddle stroke. Scraping your knuckles on a poorly placed eye ring with every downstroke of the paddle is an appropriate punishment for not thinking ahead. Use the straps to adjust the angle of the seat back, bringing it forward for a more aggressive position or reclining it for a more laid-back style. These straps will also move the seat forward and back in the cockpit, letting you adjust the angle of your legs in the foot blocks. In fact, while fishing at anchor,

I've been known to completely loosen the front straps on my Surf to Summit seat, lean back, close my eyes, and drift off.

In addition to the extra padding available in an aftermarket seat, some anglers need more cushioning for long days on the water. Although many variations on the butt pad are commercially available—from permanently mounted gel models to removable foam pads—I use a ½-inch-thick piece of closed-cell foam that I get at my local home-and-garden store. This pad not only gives me the extra cushioning that my skinny rear needs, but it lifts my cheeks off the bottom of the seat well and out of any water that might have collected there. A small piece of foam is all I need to keep my backside comfy and dry—can't beat a simple solution to a difficult problem.

The Dreaded Center Hatch

Forward of the seat, many boats have a center hatch designed to offer access to the inside of the hull and limited dry storage. Coupled with a hatch sock or cup, this is a great place to keep things that you don't use often but might need in a pinch. One of my Prowlers has a center hatch that I use to store extra rod and paddle leashes. It also comes in handy when installing eye loops and other accessories within reach of the hole.

The problem with these hatches is that they also give water a great way to enter the boat. Since this opening is situated between the angler's legs, no matter how securely these hatches are sealed, they always seem to leak. Some center hatch covers even pop off and allow water to quickly fill the boat. Many anglers prefer to permanently seal these hatches with silicone to avoid sinking at sea.

Rings and Things

Between the paddler and the foot wells, most boats have molded-in cup holders and recesses for the flotsam and jetsam of fishing. Some have factory-installed bungees designed to hold tackleboxes or the paddle. You'll want to custom-arrange eye loops, cam locks, and cleats to suit your needs. Again, make sure the placement of these items doesn't impede paddling, fishing, or landing fish.

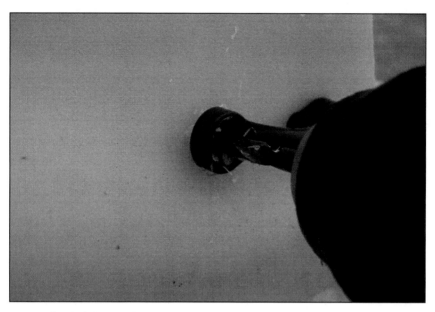

To install a deck loop with a rivet, first drill a hole through the hull just large enough to accept the rivet.

Load a rivet into the rivet gun.

Place the rivet in the predrilled hole and squeeze the handle of the gun until the rivet comes tight and the metal pin in the rivet snaps off.

Paddle Security

Between rigging tackle, casting baits, catching, fighting, and landing fish, you have a lot to think about on the water. Still, you must always keep one brain cell focused on the paddle, remaining constantly aware of its location and position. Most fishing kayaks include a paddle holder to secure the paddle while you're resting. This is an important feature, because it will secure the paddle out of the way while you fish. Space in the cockpit is at a premium; any room taken up by the paddle shaft could be better filled with rods, rigs, and fish. When you're landing a large fish, strap the paddle to the side of the boat to make room in the cockpit for your dinner guest. An angry fish thrashing in the cockpit can quickly kick the paddle into the water, suddenly changing the rules of the fishing game.

Another way to keep the paddle in the boat is a paddle leash. Securing the paddle to a paddle keeper helps you keep track of it, but a paddle leash will ensure that your motor stays with your boat.

However, a paddle leash is not idiot-proof and should only be used under limited circumstances and conditions. First, if the paddle falls overboard—even one attached to a leash—the effects of current and waves on your kayak as it drags this double-bladed brake can cause it to flip or the leash to come loose. Paddling any distance with a paddle leash attached is not only awkward but superfluous—why do you need the paddle leash if you're holding on to the paddle? Most important—*do not use a paddle leash in the surf!* Paddling through the surf with a leash attached could have deadly consequences. In the event of a wipeout, you can become hopelessly entangled in the heavy cord running from boat to paddle. What seems like a good idea at first (tethering your leash to your boat under heavy seas) will turn into a bad idea when the boat flips. Instead, concentrate on keeping hold of your paddle in the event of an ejection.

The best time to use the paddle leash is when you're actively fishing and your hands are full of rods, reels, and fish. Another time is at anchor, when the paddle could slip away unnoticed and drift off before you can recover it. Watching my paddle float off in one direction while I helplessly drift off in another is one of those recurring kayak nightmares that wakes me in the middle of the night.

Electronics

Another recurring kayak nightmare involves accidentally dropping my expensive electronics into the water and watching them silently slip below the surface then sink to the bottom. You can choose to bring along inexpensive tackle, but there's no such thing as inexpensive electronics. Lose a GPS, fishfinder, or VHF overboard, and it is going to hurt. Bad.

For that reason I've chosen electronics that are attached to the boat with bolts, lock washers, and threaded shafts. I don't trust push-button bases for my electronics. I've gone as far as tethering my GPS to an eye loop mounted in the plastic of my kayak.

When choosing where to mount electronics, try to pick a place that is in reach yet out of the way. Again, satisfying both criteria might be impossible: *Out of the way* may not be *in reach*, and vice versa. On my Prowler, I've chosen to mount my fishfinder and GPS on the raised platform at the end of each foot well. My fishfinder stands just beyond my left foot; my GPS is stationed at the end of my right leg. Although not an arm's length away, they are close enough to see. On the one hand, I can't reach these units without shimmying forward in my seat, but on the other I can't knock them in the water—and they don't take the abuse they would in the center of my cockpit. My fishfinder has a screen large enough to be seen at a distance, and I don't mess with the buttons and settings too often anyway. I can also see my GPS easily from the end of my leg. If I'm navigating through difficult terrain, I'll move my GPS closer (while still keeping it tethered to an eye ring) where I can reach it to push the buttons and see the screen better.

These units are held with plastic brackets that swivel and turn to offer limitless opportunities for viewing. Use stainless-steel bolts and lock nuts to secure these brackets to the plastic hull. For extra added security, cut a disk out of ⅛- to ¼-inch plastic or, better yet, steel. Run the bolts for the bracket through the kayak's plastic, then through the disk of harder material, and bolt the sandwich together. This will keep the bolts from pulling through as well as preventing the bracket from pulling a huge hole out of the hull should it get knocked loose. This step isn't necessary, but it might be desirable for 'yakers who expect their boats to go through brutal beatings in the surf or on raging rivers.

Installing the fishfinder's through-hull transducer puck isn't as hard as it seems. Since the transducer puck is the business end of the fishfinder that sends the signal to the bottom, be sure to choose a location in the boat's hull that will remain below the water level even when the boat is under way. Avoid placing the puck behind scupper holes or anywhere that might leave it in the wake of turbulence, which could interfere with the data. Many anglers install the puck in their center hatch; a 'yaker without a center hatch should install it as far back below the bow hatch as is reachable.

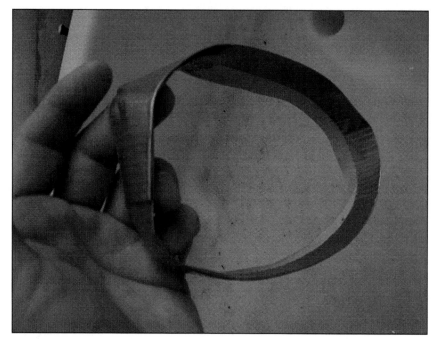

To mount a fishfinder transducer, start by making a dam out of duct tape.

The best way to install a fishfinder is by following the manufacturer's instructions. With the rise in popularity of kayak fishing, most marine electronics companies have trained their service staff to help anglers use their products with a kayak. When purchasing the fishfinder, get the standard transom-mounted transducer. The kayak's plastic is only ⅛ inch thick, so this transducer should have no problem sending a signal through the bottom. Before getting started, purchase a 12-volt 4.5-amp rechargeable gel battery from any battery store. Pick up a tube of Lexel (a clear sealant that sticks to anything and dries without leaving bubbles) at a local hardware store, and a ½-inch-thick piece of closed-cell foam—use the kneeling pads for gardeners available at any big-box home-and-garden joint. Dig around the house and find some waxed paper, a pair of scissors, and a roll of duct tape. Finally, fill a small bowl with a mixture of dish soap and water. Use a level to make sure the kayak is on a flat surface.

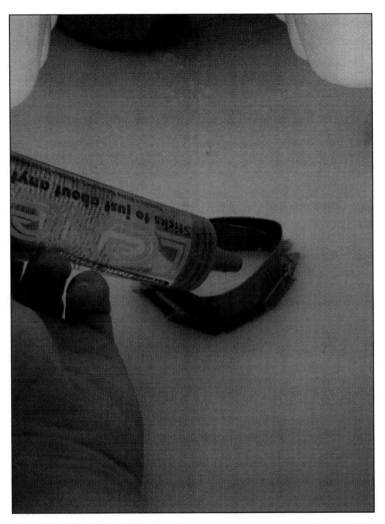

Fill the dam with ⅛ inch of Lexel.

Before starting to work inside the hull, get all the materials arranged and within easy reach. Start by spreading out a sheet of waxed paper with the waxed side up. Using the duct tape, make a circular dam by folding a length of tape—larger than the circumference of the transducer—over halfway. Bend the strip of tape around and into a loop, then tape it together. Now take another piece of tape and run it around the circumference of the dam, leaving half of the sticky side extending below the edge of the folded tape. Use the scissors to cut notches in the exposed tape, then fold the edge back. Stick the tape dam on the waxed paper, making sure the transducer will fit inside the ring with a little extra room around the side. Carefully peel the tape dam off the waxed paper and place it inside the kayak, being sure to push it down firmly against the hull so that no sealant will leak out the bottom. Cut a large hole in the nozzle of the tube of

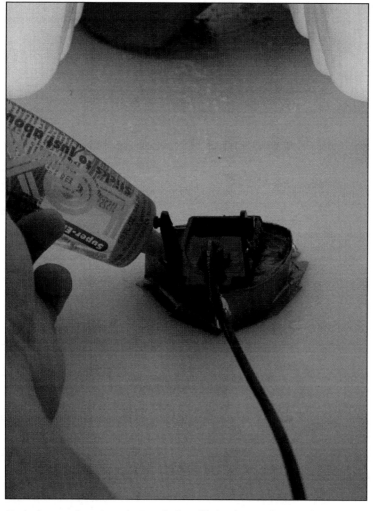

Push the transducer into the Lexel, then fill the dam to the top of the puck.

Lexel and squeeze a ⅛-inch layer of the sealant across the bottom of the tape well. Next, push the transducer into this thin layer until it almost touches the bottom of the boat. Fill the dam up to the top of the transducer puck with Lexel and let it dry. Use the soapy water to remove any sealant from your fingers. For an extra-neat job, dip a finger in the soapy water and use it to spread the sealant out around the puck. Lexel works well because it is water-resistant, doesn't break down, doesn't bubble, and is very pliable—and you won't glue your fingers together, either. Don't use epoxy. Kayaks are made of plastic, which will bend. Epoxy dries hard and will either crack or pop off the boat when twisted.

Mounting the 12-volt battery is even easier. Find a plastic food storage container (Tupperware or the like) and use the leftover Lexel to glue it to the bottom of the boat. If you can, choose a location that's closer to the center (center hatch) of the boat, where the extra weight of a battery won't be as noticeable as in the bow. Drill a hole in the container large enough to pass the battery wires through but small enough to keep too much water from leaking in. Then simply throw the battery into the container, hook up the cables, and seal the top.

Be sure to charge the battery after each trip—though a 5-amp unit will usually last half a dozen outings before it is completely spent. Also, spray all the connections with WD-40 and apply electronics gel to any sealed connections. Wrap the in-line housing in electrical tape and carry plenty of extra fuses to replace a blown unit. Also carry a couple of extra connectors to replace worn, corroded, or broken plugs.

Running cables to the battery and transducer also presents some challenges for the kayak angler. Since drilling holes in the boat can turn out badly and is always permanent, I've chosen to run my wires through my bow hatch. Granted, the installation doesn't have a clean look, and the opening does allow water splashing over the bow into the hatch. Still, I didn't have to drill any more holes in my boat (my fishfinder cable has a huge connector), and I can switch out the display unit and cables from one of my boats to another by simply purchasing a transducer puck for each hull. Of course, many anglers choose to permanently route their cables through the hull. Follow the manufacturer's instructions for such installation, and use marine-grade silicone to seal the opening completely. Be sure that the location of the fishfinder bracket will allow the cables to be routed from the display unit to the through-hull transducer and the battery.

Since the fishfinder display unit and battery will most likely be removed from the boat after each trip, make sure they're easy to disassemble, rinse off, and store. Before buying a unit, test its base for ease of release. I usually shoot the connections with WD-40 after each trip. Also, try to leave open connections suspended off the bottom of the boat and out of any water that might collect there. Take care of your gadgets and they will take care of you for years of fishing.

Rod Holders

After the tank well, the second thing that separates a fishing kayak from a regular kayak is the addition of rod holders. Whether flush mounted, bracketed, PVC, or clip-on, a fishing kayak will bristle with rod holders.

But rod holders have more uses than just holding the rod when the boat is under way or when you're fishing more than one rig. They can save the rod and the angler. Continuing on the theme *A place for everything and everything in its place*, rod holders keep rods in their place and out of the way. This saves the expensive tackle from getting banged and bruised while knocking around the cockpit and can save your quiver from getting lost in the event that the boat flips. I've turtled my kayak in the surf, turned it back over, and found all the rods still in their holders even though none was tethered. Amazing!

Also, by keeping rods and their attached hooks elevated and out of the way, there is less chance of getting injured or tangled in lines. Keep the hooks stuck in a hook guard or the first eye of the rod, not dangling from the top eye or swinging free. Be sure that the line is taut and the drag on the reel is tightened to keep the hook from swinging and piercing something.

The placement and arrangement of these rod holders will reflect their intended use. Anglers who troll will want flush-mounted holders facing the rear; those who drift may want more rod holders turned toward the side of the boat. Anglers who travel light may want fewer holders, while folks who go hard will want more. Balancing flush-mounted, vertical, and adjustable holders will allow you to address all the types of fishing you may do.

Flush Mounts

Flush-mounted rod holders, as the name implies, are mounted flat against the boat's deck. The tube that holds the rod's butt is angled under the deck, allowing you to secure the rod but not providing anything that could get in the way of fishing.

The problem with flush mounts is that they're permanent additions to the boat. These rod holders cannot be adjusted once they're

Flush-mounted rod holders angled out (like the ones behind this angler) allow you to soak baits at anchor.

installed, so do it right the first time. Also, they require a 2-inch hole to be drilled in the deck, which is never a good thing.

Still, if you plan to do a lot of trolling or soaking baits at anchor, there is no way to avoid flush-mounted rod holders. I have four of them on my Ocean Kayak Prowler. Two in the bow are angled just shy of 90 degrees; two in the stern, just over 45 degrees.

To install a flush mount, start by making sure you have all the appropriate hardware. Find rod holders that do not have a hard plastic flange round the top of the tube. The opening to the holder should be a smooth transition from the collar—a flange only serves to tear up the rod's butt.

Close the bottom of the holder's tube with a Bearing Buddy cap (the kind used on trailers). These caps are available at any boating supply store and most big-box joints. Apply a bead of Lexel to the end of the tube, then twist on the Bearing Buddy cap—this will keep water from entering the kayak through your rod holder.

Before drilling any holes, find a flat place on the boat. Make sure there's enough clearance belowdeck to accommodate the rod tube. Also, there must be enough room below the tube for the screws that attach the rod holder to pass through. There should also be enough room for your hands and any tools to work. That's a lot of room for a kayak, but it's important to think through such considerations before drilling.

If you're installing two rod holders, measure across the deck, then figure out the distance between the holders and mark with a pencil where each should be placed.

Now comes the hard part—drilling a 2½-inch hole in the kayak. Ouch.

Even though the tube for the rod is only 2¼ inches wide, you must have a 2½-inch hole saw to accommodate the angle of the tube. Measure the boat again, take a deep breath, and drill through the hull. Keep the plastic disk that is left over—it will come in handy as extra material for repairs.

Place the rod holder in the hole and stick a rod in the holder. Now sit in the kayak and turn the tube to determine what angle the rod should be pointing. I turned my forward holders out to keep my baits spread when I'm anchored. My rear holders are angled in toward the boat to troll two lures behind me. Once you've settled on an effective angle, take the rod out of the holder and mark the holes with a pencil. Apply a bead of Lexel around the base to seal out any water and secure the holder to the kayak. Then, using bolts wide enough to fill the holes and just long enough to pass through the plastic and the nut, attach the holder to the boat. Be sure to use lock washers or lock nuts to keep the bolts from backing off. If the flush-mounted rod holder comes off the boat while you're on the water, the consequences could be very bad.

Vertical Rod Holders

Although flush-mounted rod holders are great for trolling, soaking chunks at anchor, or drifting, they are not meant for holding the rods while you paddle to the fishing hole. With rods sticking off the side of the boat, I always seem to run into things, get tangled in the lines, or whack myself in the head when I get out of the boat. Plus, these are not the most secure rod holders; if you hit the reel with your paddle or turn the boat too far on its side, the rods will fall out and be lost forever.

To carry rods from point A to point B, use vertical rod holders. These can be as simple as a 2-foot-long piece of 2½-inch PVC pipe, or as fancy as a factory-made rod holder. The key feature is that the holder keep the rod securely upright, out of the way and out of the water.

To make a simple rod holder out of PVC pipe, first measure the butt of the rod. This is usually 2 feet long—though if you'll be transporting surf rods, you may want to go up to 3 feet. To accommodate the typical spinning and casting gear, a 2-inch piece of PVC will do, but if you'll be using heavy tackle you may want to bump up to 2½-inch tubing. To carry fly-fishing tackle, use a jigsaw to cut a 1-inch-wide slit in the PVC that will accommodate the fly rod's low reel seat.

To make vertical rod holders out of PVC, first measure the butt of the fishing rod.

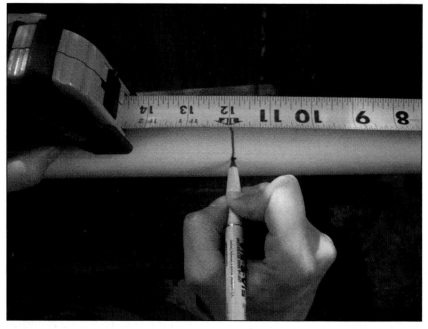

Mark the PVC at the appropriate length.

Use a jigsaw to cut the pipe.

Then use heavy-duty zip ties to attach the rod holder to your office crate. To secure the rod, either drill a hole in the PVC and clip on a Surf to Summit rod leash, or simply run a bungee cord from one side of the crate, over the reels and through the lines, to the other side of the crates.

To get fancy, purchase a premade triple rod holder from a boating supply store and attach it to your office crate. These holders are great because they have a molded flange that is easier on the rod's cork or foam butt. Also, these factory-made holders include precut crevices to hold lures, hooks, rigs, pliers, and scissors. Place the unit along the outside of the crate. Take a piece of soft plastic or ⅛-inch-thick pressure-treated plywood and place it on the inside of the crate. Run the bolts for the rod holder through the crate and plywood, then bolt them on tightly. Again, drill a small hole in each holder and attach a rod leash or run a bungee around the unit to secure the rods.

Zip ties will hold the rod holder in your milk crate.

Adjustable Rod Holders

The best of both worlds—fishing and transporting—is an adjustable rod holder. Two companies have cornered the market on this product: Scotty and RAM Mounts. Each of these rod holders accomplishes the same objective in a slightly different way. The Scotty holder uses a ratcheting connection between the rod holder and its base, and the base and the boat, allowing you to lock your rod into a limited number of positions. The RAM Mount, on the other hand, uses a ball and clamp to allow infinite adjustment.

Both systems have their most important qualities in common: They're adjustable, removable, and damn near indestructible.

The cool thing about these holders is that they offer a million and one ways to hold a fishing rod. Each starts with a base that can be mounted to the kayak at more than one position (vertical, horizontal, or standing), allowing you to insert the riser at several angles. Next, the system's riser can accommodate more than one type of accessory—a rod holder, a navigation light, even a platform for electronics. The rod holder can be turned, twisted, and tilted then locked into place to hold the rod perfectly. Each company has designed a variety of risers, holders, and bases to fit nearly any application.

Not only are these holders easy to install, they're easy to remove. Even though the standard base sticks up only an inch, each company offers a flush-mounted base that leaves nothing for lines to catch when the holder is not in use. As you switch from one type of fishing to another, you can move or remove holders to best serve your needs. Pretty spiffy.

I have one Scotty holder mounted in my cockpit, between my feet, at arm's length. Most of the time I don't use it; I prefer to keep it at home and out of the way. When I'm soaking chunk baits or fishing for big game and need more than one rod, however, I'll attach the Scotty holder and instantly have a third hand.

Precariously sticking up out of my boat, that rod holder has been smacked, cracked, and whacked a million times a million ways and never even chipped. What is that stuff made of?

I don't use adjustable holders for trolling or soaking baits, though, because they leave the rod butt sticking into the cockpit. I prefer flush-mounted holders for this application—the rod butts extend below the deck, where they don't get in the way. Some guys attach bases around their boat then move the rod holders where they need them. Two bases attached on either side of the tank well will carry rods pointing at an angle or parallel to the boat so you can pass under heavy cover. Other anglers use the extended arm for their rod holder and attach a section of swimming-pool noodle foam to hold hooks and rigs. Many 'yakers use their RAM Mount to hold electronics; this works great in tight places where deck space may be at a premium.

Adjustable rod holders come in enough shapes and styles to ensure that there's a unit to meet every angler's needs.

Anchor Trolley

Kayak anglers are master problem solvers, and anchoring a kayak is no small problem to solve. The problem is, if you throw out an anchor and secure the line to the side, your kayak will turn its side to the current, leaving it unstable and quickly flipping you into the water. The answer, of course, is to run the anchor off the bow or stern. Since kayaks are elliptical, you can secure it with either of the boat's pointy ends turned into the current. Since they're unstable, reaching the bow or stern to secure an anchor is more dangerous than anchoring side-to the current.

If only there were a way to run the anchor to the bow or stern from the cockpit. If only . . .

Enter the anchor trolley. No one knows who cooked up this ingenious answer—though many 'yakers take credit for it—but it has opened up a great deal of kayak fishing opportunities.

To build an anchor trolley, start with a length of 5-millimeter rope slightly longer than twice the length of your kayak. In other words, if the kayak is 15 feet long—get 35 feet of rope. Then purchase four stainless-steel eye loops, six small stainless carabiners, and enough rivets to attach the eye loops to the deck. Be sure that the rivets fit through the eye loop grommets, and also that the carabiner will fit through the eye loop when it's secured to a flat surface.

Attach an eye loop to the bow of the boat, two at midship, and another at the stern. Next, clip a carabiner to each eye loop. To get fancy, replace the carabiners with small 5mm pulleys—the kind used on sailboats. Cut the rope in half. Take one half and run it from the bow carabiner to the midship carabiner and back. Tie a carabiner

The anchor trolley. One carabiner runs the anchor line to the bow, while the other runs it to the stern.

between the two ends of the rope using a bowline knot. Do the same from the stern carabiner to midship and back, tying the remaining carabiner in the middle.

There are three basic types of anchor available to 'yakers, and each has its specific uses. You might think that a light, low-profile kayak would be easy to anchor—but exactly because this plastic boat is light and low-profile, it's more difficult to apply the force required to drive an anchor into the sand or rocks.

For deep-water anchoring, I use a small 4-pound Danforth anchor that features two flat tines hinging on a metal shaft. I'll add 4 or 5 feet of chain to the anchor in water over 30 feet deep or where I expect to encounter swift current. In shallow or calm water, I go with a 4-pound Bruce anchor, which is shaped like a cupped fist and easily digs into soft bottom. Anglers fishing swift-moving rivers with rocky bottoms will be best served by a folding grapple anchor. Attach the anchor rope to the front loop on the blade end of the grapple, then zip-tie the rope to the loop on the end of the shaft. This way, if the anchor gets stuck in the rocks, simply pull hard, break the zip tie, free the rope, and pull the anchor out in the opposite direction that it went into the structure.

The rule of thumb when it comes to the length of the anchor rope is: *Take three times as much rope as the expected water depth.* If you'll be fishing in 20 feet of water, be sure to have 60 feet of rope. I carry two sections of rope in my car—a 100-foot length and a 50-foot piece. In general, you can't have too much rope. Depending on depth, current, and sea conditions, you might need 50 feet to anchor in 10 feet of water. Always slide a foam crab pot buoy onto the rope so that you can recover it if you have to break anchor or lose the connection.

Anchoring in a kayak is an exercise in controlled chaos. Things happen very quickly and steps must be followed carefully; otherwise you could lose the anchor and rope or flip the kayak.

To anchor with the bow facing into the current, start by making sure the anchor rope is clear and untangled, lying in loose loops over one leg. Then chuck the anchor over the side of the boat, followed by the sliding buoy. After the anchor hits the bottom, but before it can dig in, tie an overhand knot in the rope to keep the buoy from sliding off the rope. Clip the rope in the carabiner that's tied in the middle of the trolley line looped to the bow, and quickly run the rope to the front of the boat—like raising a flag on a flagpole. Once the carabiner hits the bow eye, come tight on the rope and secure it to a cam or cleat.

Anchoring is one of the most precarious procedures for any boater—especially kayakers. There are many dangers inherent in securing your boat against the forces of wind and current. Always exercise extreme caution.

Take a Stand

Anglers fishing the clear, shallow waters of the Gulf Coast, Florida's Atlantic side, or the northeastern flats can't stand to sit while fishing. When sight casting to skinny-water fish, the higher you are off the water, the better you can see into it. From a seated position, on a good day, I can see fish 20 feet around my boat. When I'm standing, that distance triples. If the water is bumpy and I can't stand up in my kayak, I'll sit on the crate behind my seat for a better view.

Standing and sight fishing are so important in the clear-water states that anglers have started using portable, removable outriggers to steady their kayaks (see Gulf Coast in chapter 6). Since paddling against the resistance of two booms and two skegs is a real drag, a set of outriggers should be easy to assemble and disassemble as well as small enough to store in a center hatch. However, the unit must be strong enough to withstand the forces of wind and water while steadying the kayak against the tottering of a full-grown adult. Carry the broken-down stabilizers to the fishing grounds; once you're on the scene, pull them out, put them together, and install them on the boat.

Scotty Plastics offers a set of outriggers that feature two super-strong aluminum booms and a pair of inflatable bladders. The system breaks down to fit in the kayak's hatch; it's then easy to assemble and inflate when needed. The nice thing about the Scotty stabilizers is that they can be inserted into a standard Scotty mount—which means that the same base can host rod holders or stabilizers, depending on the situation. Add a set of bases to the bow and a set to the stern, and you can move the outriggers in front of or behind you as needed.

Even though most kayaks are designed to be stable and maneuverable while the driver is standing (see the Pedal Power section in chapter 1), a set of kayak outriggers will ensure that you stay in your 'yak.

Live Wells

Probably the ultimate kayak fishing accessory is a high-volume live well. With a full array of electronics, lights, rod holders, dry storage, *and* a circulating live bait system, the only difference between a motorboat and a paddle boat is the motor.

Fortunately, most kayak anglers can get away without using live bait. Even if you used minnows to catch flounder or shiners to catch perch in your previous life as a powerboater, do everything you can to avoid live bait on the kayak. Not only are most live bait systems cumbersome and unreliable, but paddling around a gallon or two of water is a drag.

Big fish are often caught on live bait. The minnow bucket behind the author carried the eels that fooled this striper.

With the introduction of super-scented artificial baits like Gulp! and Fishbites, I've done away with natural bait completely. No more pumping, freezing, thawing, cutting, or smelling bait: I simply open a package, apply the bait to my hook, and go.

Still, some anglers are sticklers for livies, and others can't avoid using the real deal. California's saltwater fishery is dependent on live bait, for instance, and nothing fools a Florida sailfish like a live pogy or bluerunner dangling on the surface. For them, there are some amazing kayak-friendly live bait systems.

For most live bait applications, a simple Frabill Flow Troll bait bucket will carry mummichogs, shiners, finger mullet, and even small croaker or spot. Some 'yakers have gone to using a mesh bait bag that can be folded flat and stored in the hatch. The Flow Troll takes up more space on the boat but will hold water while you're under way. The mesh bag is lighter and easier to store, but it must stay in the water, where it can drag against the kayak. Another option growing in popularity among 'yakers is a homemade bait tube. Simply take a 2-foot section of 2-inch PVC tubing and seal each end with a cap. Drill holes in the cap and connect a piece of thin rope. Fill the tube with baits and keep it in the water to keep the baits alive. The tube must be submerged to be effective, but the hydrodynamic torpedo-like design reduces drag and makes the system work.

For larger baits or longer trips, a self-contained bait bucket will be necessary. I use a system designed by Marine Metal Products that combines a water-resistant aerator and a collapsible soft-sided bucket. However, live bait enthusiasts will point out that, for many types of baitfish, aeration can actually harm the critters, knocking off their slime coat and not recirculating the wastewater.

For master baiters, there is only one way to go: a circulating live bait well that constantly pumps in fresh water and pumps out dirty water. Again, California kayak anglers have taken the lead with this technology. Several companies offer professionally designed and constructed live bait wells. Although each is as unique as the angler who cooked it up, all of these systems have basic elements in common.

The first considerations are the size of the tank and the type of bait you'll be holding captive. Some baits need more water and more current, while others enjoy swimming in a circle. Then measure the tank well on the kayak to be sure that a given tank will fit—some kayak manufacturers have even designed their tank wells to accept certain live bait systems. Check with your kayak outfitter to learn what systems work best in what boats.

There are several key factors to look for in a bait well. First, the pump should be indestructible, submersible, and powerful. All electrical connections should be water-resistant. The system should run on the same 12-volt battery that charges your kayak's fishfinder. Look for a toggle switch to turn the system on and off while you're on the

A kayak, like a dog, tends to resemble its owner. This simply layout is utilitarian and minimalist. An experienced kayaker doesn't need capricious electronics. A small minnow bucket and battery-operated aerator keep bait alive. The crate is mounted above the tank well to keep its contents dry and provide more storage beneath it. A plastic grocery bag holds an extra sweatshirt, while a small shower radio provides entertainment.

water. The inlet nozzle should be angled to shoot water around the sides of the well, while the outlet tube should exit from the bottom of the tank to drain the water and empty the tank quickly. Be sure that there are stainless-steel screens on the ends of the inlet and outlet tubes to keep debris from clogging the system.

Sure, nothing beats live bait for "matching the hatch," and with a little ingenuity—or a little cash—kayak anglers can take the plunge.

Navigational Lights

If you 'yak at night, you'll want a battery-operated navigation light. Although many versions of these lights are available at boating supply stores and big-box outlets, the rigors (and associated dangers) of

This boat is loaded for bear. A soft-sided cooler holds the day's bait. A hard/soft cooler provides dry storage inside an office crate. Four PVC rod holders carry the weapons of fish destruction. Check out the anchor trolley. The ropes stretching from midship to the stern carry the anchor rope back to hold the stern into the current, while the loop from midship to the bow carries it forward.

kayaking demand something better. Most nocturnal anglers are using a Scotty SEA-Light—a 360-degree navigation light that runs for eight hours on two AA batteries.

The light is sealed against water and practically indestructible. It's also highly visible—I can usually see colleagues fishing 2 miles or more away. The best navigation lights for kayaks will feature a lamp that won't blind you but is visible from a distance. My light is removable so it can be clipped to a life vest in case of an emergency. The system comes with a 20-inch pole, which holds the light high enough to be seen over the waves but not so high that it gets caught on overhead obstructions. It also comes with one of Scotty's 241 mounts, which allows me to attach it almost anywhere on my boat.

Since I don't like drilling holes in my kayak, I've drilled holes in my crate and attached the mount to the plastic supports.

Even anglers who fish during the day would be served by a navigational light. Foggy conditions can reduce visibility, and a light will make you more visible to boaters. Also, dawn and dusk patrols require lighting—and you never know when you might get caught out after dark. And don't forget about solar eclipses!

By using the Scotty system or a similar setup, the nav light can become a permanent fixture on your boat. That way you'll have it when you need it.

Kayak Repair

I've already told you the story of day my kayak took on water and almost sank (see Pumps in chapter 2 if you really have to go through the gory details again). I made it to the beach in one piece, where I inspected the hull and found a small gash. No bigger than a keyhole, it was undoubtedly the result of years of dragging my boat across parking lots and launch ramps. My abusive behavior had caught up with me.

I was able to temporarily patch the hole on site with superglue, which I carry just in case, and return to the launch ramp. Safe at home, I began to do some research on kayak repair.

Avoidable or not, accidents happen. Plastic is tough, but it isn't impenetrable. Whether you drill an unnecessary aperture in the deck or grind an unnoticed gash in the hull—holes happen. But holes in a plastic boat are not its death knell. They're actually easy to fix.

After Googling "kayak repair" I discovered a tool called a plastic welder available at www.kayakfishingstuff.com. Fifty bucks and a few days later I had the gadget, a couple of pieces of plastic, and a sheet of wire mesh waiting at my doorstep.

Referring to the instructions included with the welder and those found on kfs.com, I plunged into the project with confidence.

First, I cleaned the area to be repaired with soap and water to remove all the grit and grunge that had been ground into my keel. Then I propped the boat onto a couple of sawhorses to bring it up to working height, and used a level to make sure it was flat and straight.

I plugged in the plastic welder. The thing looks like a soldering iron except the tip is smashed into a flat, round wand. While I waited for the welder to heat up, I scrounged around in my workshop for some discarded pieces of plastic left over from holes I had cut and drilled in my boat for rod holders and hatches. I decided to use original plastic from my kayak rather than the rods provided with the welder in hopes of maintaining the consistency and color of the original material.

I cut the plastic into small 1- to 2-inch chunks and used a pair of needle-nose pliers to hold each piece to the area that needed repair. After heating the kayak hull until the plastic started to soften, I turned the welder onto my piece of patch to warm that up, too. Then I held the two together and pressed the welder into the little plastic chunk until it softened to the consistency of cold cream cheese. Once the plastic was malleable, I used the flattened end of the welder to spread it over the damaged area. As one piece of plastic melted into the hull, I'd add another and another until the worn-down section of my keel was built back up to its original height.

When the plastic dried, it had the same color and consistency of the surrounding material—you can hardly tell there's a patch. My kayak was back to better-than-new condition.

One word . . . *plastic.*

Stow and Go

The best thing about kayak fishing is its simplicity: Kayaks are simple to own, simple to operate, simple to carry, and simple to store. In fact, these last two qualities are particularly important to low-impact anglers. A kayak can be carried almost anywhere, launched, recovered, and then stored almost anywhere. Simple.

I know guys who keep their kayaks in their apartments. I've launched a kayak by lowering it with a rope from a dock. I've seen anglers trailering a kayak with a bicycle, and I know guys whose kayaks are permanent parts of their car. Some anglers are even mother-shipping their 'yaks with powerboats to distant fishing grounds. A kayak can go anywhere and fish anytime.

With the correct accessories, a kayak can be an unstoppable fishing machine. Starting with storage, a 'yak can be crammed, jammed, hung, or laid almost anywhere. My kayak is either on top of my car or lying in my front yard. After four years exposed to the elements, it's a little faded, but it still works just fine.

The best storage place for a boat is indoors. Several companies produce straps designed to hang a 'yak from garage rafters. Wheeleez has a set of straps that can be linked together like a chain to hold more than one boat. Other companies produce kayak hoists—the ultimate storage option. These allow you to drive your car into the garage, unstrap your boat, hook the bow and stern to the hoist's ropes, then lift the boat to the ceiling and secure it with a cleat. Time to go fishing? Just drive up, lower the boat, strap it down, and off you go.

'Yak anglers with enough room and enough money can purchase kayak trailers. These units are just like regular boat trailers, only smaller. They allow you to launch and recover your boat without dragging or lifting it. Most of these trailers also have lockable storage boxes so you can store seat, life vest, paddle, even rods, reels, and tackle on the trailer. This is the best way to pamper a kayak.

Unfortunately, few fishing kayaks see this kind of treatment. Instead they're dragged, dropped, and jimmied into some ugly situations. The best method for transporting a kayak is a pickup truck. With some wedging and strapping, an 8-foot bed will accommodate kayaks up to 16 feet. Bed extenders like those made by Thule and Yakima will support the kayak as it sticks out of the back of a truck.

Guys who aren't rich enough to afford a trailer or lucky enough to have a pickup will have to find a way to load their kayak on top of their car. I've been wrestling my boat onto my jeep for years. Thanks to my Yakima racks, I can easily load and unload two kayaks by myself. The key to this system is the BoatLoader bar. This bar pulls out of the rack's crossbar and provides an extra set of "hands" when I'm loading my boat.

First, I pull the boat parallel with my jeep. Then I extend the BoatLoader from the front rack, lift the bow of my boat, and lean it on the bar. While the boat rests with its bow in the air, I move to the stern, lift, and pivot the back of the boat onto the rear set of LandShark Saddles. Next, I move to the bow, lift it, and turn it onto the forward rack. I make sure to position the kayak so that the logo on the side or handle is centered between the bars. If I have a second kayak to load, I pivot the first boat onto the far set of racks, strap it down, prethread the second set of straps, then repeat the process. Finally, I retract the BoatLoader and pull out my kayak straps. Both Yakima and Thule offer a variety of ingenious ways to get a kayak from the ground to the roof of a car.

A quality set of straps makes loading and unloading the boat easier, not to mention safer. The most important part is the cam. A quality cam will be made of corrosion-resistant metal and feature a heavy spring. Look for a web strap that is thick and stiff. Not only is a stronger strap more secure, but it's easy to work with. Thinner straps are harder to throw over the boat and more difficult to feed through the cam. Go with the best you can buy.

Standing beside the car, starting with either the bow or stern crossbar, throw the tag end of the strap over the car and let it fall on the other side of the boat. Then run around the car, grab the tag end, pass it under the crossbar, and throw it back over the boat. Adjust the length of the straps until the cam is lying on the flattest part of the kayak's side. Thread the tag end under the rack's tower and crossbar, run it through the cam, tighten until the kayak is snug but not being crushed, and weave any extra strap material around the base of the rack.

To be ultra super safe, tie down the bow and stern, too. In windy conditions or when you're traveling long distances, be sure to run a piece of parachute cord from the bow of the boat to the front bumper of the car, and another piece from the stern to the rear bumper. I keep a couple of pieces of precut, pretied cord in my car for just such situations.

To secure the kayak to your rack and prevent theft, use a bike cable and a combination lock. Thread the cable through the scuppers and around the rack's crossbar to slow a thief down. Several companies make lock systems specifically designed for kayaks and other sports equipment. The LashLock, for instance, allows you to replace your strap with a steel cable and your cam with a combination lock.

But getting the kayak from the garage to the car is only half the journey—you still have to get the boat from the car to the water. Doing that usually involves dragging and lugging it across asphalt, through grass, over concrete, and through the sand. A kayak cart makes this much easier.

It's a good idea to buy a kayak cart when you buy your kayak. After all, it is an essential accessory, and if you're already making a big investment it doesn't hurt to make it a little bigger. Just like everything else in 'yaking, it pays to buy the best cart you can find. Also, just like everything else in 'yaking, if you don't want to buy it, you can make it.

As I've mentioned previously, I'd rather spend money than time on my kayak. Once you buy all the components for a homemade cart—well, you could have a factory jobby for only a few bucks more. Besides, the type of cart I need for beach launching isn't buildable using components from the local big-box hardware store. To launch on the beach or go ATV with your kayak, you've got to have a Wheeleez cart—there is no substitute.

The key feature to these carts is their oversized, underinflated balloon tires. Skinnier tires just won't cut it. Not only are these carts unsurpassed in the sand, they're the best over the river and through the woods, too. The big tires distribute the weight of the kayak over a larger area, making it easier to roll across soft or uneven terrain. The low-pressure tires also serve as suspension, allowing me to cross rough ground or even roll up curbs and over parking blocks.

Much of the fishing I do involves driving along the shore until I locate birds diving over schools of feeding fish. Then, before the fish can sound and the birds fly off, I have to unload the boat, load it on the cart, and rush across the beach. If I can keep my kayak fully loaded with rods, rigs, and electronics, it makes my response time that much faster. Besides, whenever I can move all of my stuff at once without having to return to the car for more, I've saved steps and time.

Look for a cart that can be broken down and stored in the kayak's day hatch. The cart should therefore be light enough to carry and small enough to fit in the trunk of a car. It should be tough enough to support the weight of a fully loaded kayak as it bumps and bounces over impossible obstacles.

For anglers who don't require a tank to move their kayak, a homemade cart will do. There are many plans for kayak carts—some complex, some simple—but almost all require PVC tubing. The simplest PVC carts are shaped like an H; the top two tines go through the scupper holes below the kayak's tank well, and each of the bottom tines is attached to a tire. Add another crossbar below the middle support and use a piece of aluminum tubing for an axle. Find some lawn tractor tires at a local tool supply store that fit the aluminum tubing and drill a small hole in each end of the tubing to accept a pin. Drop a length of aluminum tubing down each arm of the H for added support, then seal the ends of the PVC with gobs of silicone. Glue the whole thing together with PVC primer, then sealant.

The best thing about this type of kayak cart is that when you unload the kayak, you can flip the cart upside down and insert the tines in the stern scuppers with the wheels sticking out of the tank well. That lets you use the cart to take the kayak with you, then use the kayak to take the cart with you.

Which is, after all, one of the biggest advantages of kayak fishing. Go anywhere, anytime, anyhow. With a set of roof racks and a kayak cart, you'll be surprised where you can take your kayak and where your kayak will take you.

The Fashionable 'Yaker

Of course, it's not enough for anglers to simply *be good*, they've got to *look* good, too. The days of cutoff jeans and a bloodstained T-shirt are over. Today's fashion-conscious angler must match pastels and coordinate accessories to put together a look that is fashionable and functional.

All kidding aside—there is more at stake when dressing to kayak fish than making a fashion faux pas. In fact, in extreme heat or extreme cold, wearing the wrong thing could lead to a very bad experience. Moreover, modern clothing systems allow you to extend the season—and range—into realms you may have previously considered unfishable.

I've fished on nights when seawater froze into a glaze on my kayak, and days when 90-degree heat and 90 percent humidity boiled my brain. But because I dress right, these conditions are both bearable and fishable.

STAY DRY

I hate to get wet! Okay, sounds strange coming from a lifelong water baby, but I can't stand being wet and sticky and sandy and gritty and funky. While on the water I do everything I can to stay out of the water. I wear waders much later in the season than necessary. I wear a dry top much longer than necessary. For me, the trick to being comfortable is staying dry. Indeed, whether facing extreme heat or extreme cold, dry anglers are usually happy anglers.

The first step to staying dry is an impervious outer layer of waterproof/breathable fabric. From head to toe, I'm covered in a full-body condom. On top: a dry top. Down below: a pair of waders. In spring and fall it's breathable GoreTex. In winter—super-insulated neoprene. Only in the heat of summer will you find me wallowing in my kayak, but you won't find me wallowing in the water.

Now a word of warning. Old salts will say that wearing waders in water that is more than chest-deep is a tragedy waiting to happen. Many outdoorsmen have been lost forever when their waders filled and they were dragged down into the freezing depths. But the correct combination of waders, dry top, and PFD should prevent this catastrophe from befalling a kayak angler.

DRY TOP AND WADERS

In fact, this system has been tested under controlled conditions and found effective. To test cold-weather wear, a bunch of my buddies rented a swimming pool and practiced tipping and reentering their kayaks. Half the guys were in waders, half in dry suits. They discovered that as long as you're able to remount your boat within a few minutes, the wader/dry top combination is effective. A prolonged separation from the kayak, however, will lead to water leaking into the waders. You'll be soaked, and you might sink.

I'm not one for controlled circumstances; I've tested the system under circumstances that were most definitely out of control. One fateful New Year's Eve, for example, my best fishing buddy Kevin Whitley and I decided to chase big stripers on Diamond Shoals off North Carolina's Outer Banks. Never mind that we had never paddled the shoals. Never mind that this stretch of water is unaffectionately known as the Graveyard of the Atlantic. All Kevin and I saw were big striped bass and glory.

We arrived at the beach predawn, readied our 'yaks, and dragged them through the shore break. As soon as we hit the water, the wind started to blow 15 knots out of the southwest. *Never mind—I thought—the seas are still manageable, and we're less than a mile from the beach.* Then I saw an angler in a surf boat land a 40-inch striper on his first cast with a pencil popper. My attention turned to the waves breaking on the shoals where the striper were lurking. I paddled close and made a cast with a bucktail. Before I could retrieve my lure, the current and wind pushed me into the maul, and I had to quickly recover my boat and paddle toward deeper water and safety. I tried another cast, but was again swept into the surf. Waves were coming from every direction, running together, exploding in front of me. I hailed Kevin with my VHF: "Let's get the hell outta here!"

"I'm already on my way," he replied.

I turned my boat and retreated for the deeper water outside the shoals, where I thought I would be safe. Once in the clear, I put away my casting rod and grabbed a heavier trolling outfit. While I had my eyes on rigging my rod with a big swimming plug, I heard the sickening sound of the wind whipping spray off a wave crest. I looked up to see a chest-high breaker barreling toward me from the side. I only had a second to grab my paddle and try to turn my boat in the wave. It wasn't enough. The breaker smashed into me, throwing me from my boat into the late-December water. I emerged on the other side of the wave to find my gear bobbing in a soup of whitewater; my boat had capsized. I first grabbed my paddle, then reached across my 'yak and pulled it top-side up. Before the next roller could come in and repeat the spanking, I remounted my boat and paddled like hell for the beach.

Once safely on terra firma, I checked to make sure that I was still in one piece. I had survived my first tangle with the Graveyard, only taking a little water around the neck of my rain jacket. Pretty lucky.

Staying dry in fall and spring, when the water temperatures range from the low 60s to mid-70s with air temperatures to match, is possible thanks to high-tech fabrics that are impervious to outside water while perforated to allow body moisture to escape from within.

Although many companies make breathable fabrics, not all "breathable" fabrics are created equal. Some consist of a perforated fabric sprayed with a waterproofing substance to keep water out. Other materials are inherently breathable and waterproof. Of course the latter perform much better than the former. Whereas sprayed-on coatings eventually wear off and need reapplying, true breathable fabrics will keep you dry and comfy forever.

Yet no matter how hard you work to stay dry, water will find its way into your clothes. For most applications, a high-quality rain jacket will serve perfectly. Not only will it shed water splashed from the paddle or boat, but it will also keep you dry in the event of rain. Be sure to always pack the rain jacket into your kayak's saddle bag for emergencies.

Anglers who push the limits, launching through surf and paddling through rough seas, will need a dry top, too. One of the best is made by Aquaskinz—a company from the Northeast that field-tests its equipment in the worst fishing conditions imaginable. This outfit features neoprene gaskets around the wrists and neck and a gasket and drawstring around the waist. The rest of the top is built of lightweight, breathable material that expels perspiration while shedding water and wind. The dry top folds up and fits easily in the pack behind a kayak seat.

A good pair of gloves will keep your hands warm when wet while still allowing you to tie knots and manipulate tackle. Most fishing gloves are made of neoprene and feature convertible fingers that enable you to fish. Most of the time, I can get away with a pair of wool gloves with the fingers cut off. Aquaskinz makes a great pair of gloves, too. They are specifically designed for fishing, with neoprene backs and synthetic leather on the palms and in the fingers. The material on the tip of the pointer finger and thumb is so thin, you can tie knots, cast, even pick up swivels off the deck without having to take off your gloves.

Not only do gloves keep your hands warm—they keep 'em safe, too. Fishhooks, lines, and tackle can do a doozey on your most important appendages. I used to return from fishing barely able to bend my sliced-up fingers or close my swollen hands. Since I started wearing my A-skinz gloves, though, I can fish with impunity. In fact, the gloves even make it easier to handle slippery fish and paddles.

The key to any clothing system is comfort. A dry top or rain jacket will not keep you dry if it's back in the car because you didn't want to wear it. Weather conditions can change quickly—what you were wearing when you left the launch may not be effective halfway into a fishing trip. And if things do get bad, a rain jacket or dry top stored in the 'yak can save the day. Conversely, if conditions improve—temperatures rise or the wind lays down—an outerwear system should be easy to remove and store in the boat. Even in summer I stuff a rain jacket and pair of water-resistant pants in the bag behind my Surf to Summit seat. Moreover, in winter, temperatures can be below freezing at dawn, then rise as the sun does. That's when I can take off my dry top and store my fleece top in the same bag.

With only a few inches between you and the water and no protection from the elements, a dry top or rain jacket and pair of waders is your only chance to stay warm and dry. With the proper combination of outer garments, you can extend your kayak fishing season through the winter and into the worst conditions.

COLD-WEATHER OUTFITTING

Admittedly, a kayak dry suit is the best system for staying warm and safe on the water. This is the setup preferred by whitewater 'yakers— and if it's good enough for them, it's more than good enough for us. Whereas a dry top/waders combo offers the opportunity for water to enter the system and sink you, a dry suit is a closed unit that will let in only a little water and *not* sink you. No doubt, the dry suit is the way to go.

With a dry top and neoprene waders, a paddler is ready for the worst cold weather.

Most kayak anglers who fish through the cold months use the waders/dry top system because, in many cases, they may already employ these same components for surf fishing or hunting. Moreover, it's easy to find a pair of waders and rain jacket at any outdoors store. Still, just because this is the easiest and cheapest route doesn't mean it's the safest.

"You've got to dress for immersion," says Kokatat's Mike Duff. Without a doubt, a single-piece dry suit is the kayaker's best chance of surviving a dunking. These units are constructed of a breathable material that's both tough enough to survive the rigors of kayak fishing and soft enough to comfortably wear all day long.

The neck, legs, and ankles are sealed with neoprene gaskets. The seams are sealed with tape, thread, and glue. "A dry suit is a one-piece solution that can handle any condition," Duffy explains. "It all depends on what you wear under it." For warmer weather, he recommends light silk underwear. For the coldest conditions, "You wear a bunny suit," he says. Huh? "A bunny suit is a one-piece fleece suit," Duffy continues; "the pants won't separate from the shirt and leave a cold gap against the skin."

The key to comfort is a proper fit: "It's not a potato sack with arms and legs sewn on." In fact, there are men's and women's suits. The legs and arms are articulated to provide mobility for paddling a kayak. Each dry suit company provides clear instructions for proper sizing and fit. "Not only does the suit have to be comfortable to paddle in," Duffy goes on, "but it has to be comfortable to swim in, too."

That's the big difference between the dry suit and the waders/dry top combo. Wearing a PFD, you could conceivably swim some distance in a dry suit. In waders and a dry top, the best you can hope for is to flounder back to your boat or splash around until someone rescues you.

There is one more advantage to the dry suit. Most companies have models that include a "relief zipper" across the lower abdomen. After two cups of coffee and a 3-mile morning paddle, the advantages of this quickly become obvious. Stripping off a dry top and peeling down a pair of waders while bobbing up and down in a kayak isn't easy—or safe. In fact, this is when you're most vulnerable, because you've removed not just your protective clothing but most likely your PFD, too. The relief zipper allows male paddlers to "drain the bilge" without falling overboard. Worth its weight in gold.

Duffy puts it simply: "You've got to ask yourself what your life is worth." Weigh safety and comfort in the worst conditions against the cost of a dry suit and you'll see that this system is a great value.

But it's not enough to stay dry from the outside. An angler has to be dry on the inside, too.

Perspiration is as much the kayaker's enemy as rain or spray. Paddling into a head sea with a headwind will soak you from the outside, while doing the workout will soak you on the inside, too.

To combat perspiration, a fabric must first wick sweat from the skin, then warm the water with body heat. Some materials do this well. Wool, for instance, is the most effective natural wicking fiber. Not only does it absorb water, but it keeps you warm when it's wet. I have a pair of fingerless wool gloves that I wear when the air temperature is in the 40s and the water temperature matches. These gloves keep my hands warm even after repeated dunkings to scoop up fish.

Oh yeah, wool is a natural odor eliminator, too. Is there anything this stuff can't do?

Actually, wool has some undesirable properties as well. Some people find it itchy, and it's definitely "poofy"—prone to snagging and catching. When it comes to the popular wool socks, you can take care of the "itchy" part by simply combining them with a pair of silk liner socks.

Always itching to one-up Mother Nature, clothing companies have developed fabrics incorporating the good qualities of wool and avoiding the bad ones. Not only do these super fabrics wick sweat and warm it, but many of them are also windproof and even water-resistant. With the proper clothing, you can fish in almost any weather at any time of year.

The key to comfortable kayak fishing is dressing right. Everyone has an opinion of what specific clothing system works best. And everyone is right. All kinds of combinations are effective against cold and wet, and each one is war-torn and time-proven by its proponents.

Although I am no Inuit, breaking ice with my kayak to chase down a whale with a sharp stick, I do fish some pretty miserable conditions in relative comfort. The Chesapeake Bay is my backyard, and even in the dark of winter it's full of fish. To make things worse, these fish are most active at night. So those of us who 'yak fish the

Chesapeake are battling wet and cold—*and* struggling in the dark. I've spent whole nights sight casting to big striped bass when the water temperature was in the upper 30s and the air temperature in the upper 20s. Admittedly, my worst conditions would be a nice night for some kayak anglers in the Extreme North. The point is, my clothing system allows me to enjoy it, and there are clothing options that allow my northern cousins to do the same. All over the world, kayak fishing is a year-round sport.

When dressing for the coldest nights, I start with a pair of SmartWool socks. These socks are famous for keeping feet warm and dry even in the worst conditions. Under 5 millimeters of neoprene and a pair of heavy boots, they perform very well. Granted, anyone who pursues outdoor sports through the winter is going to have cold feet. There is no way around it. Some nights my feet get so cold, I swear they go numb and I can't feel them anymore. A good pair of socks at least eases that pain.

Above the socks, I wear a pair of long johns made of a synthetic material. These leggings feel like fleece, but they're actually a high-tech material made by Under Armour that pulls water from my skin then transfers it to the outer layer, where my body heat is able to warm it. Be sure to choose a material that inherently wicks perspiration; some products use chemical additives to lift water. These coatings eventually wear off and lose effectiveness. Not only should the individual threads of the fabric absorb water, but they should also be woven in a pattern that will aid the transfer of moisture while providing insulation. Up top, I've got on a matching turtleneck (by the same company) that does the same thing.

Over my long johns, I wear a pair of fleece pants that have stirrups to hold the legs down when I stuff my feet into my waders. On top, I wear a wool shirt made by Patagonia. But this is not your grandpa's scratchy and stiff wool shirt; it's as thin as a T-shirt but made of super-absorbent, super-insulated, super-thin wool.

After years of trial and error attempting to develop synthetic fibers that will outperform natural materials, forward-thinking clothing companies such as Patagonia are returning to the real thing.

Wool has a higher weight-to-warmth ratio than any human-made counterpart. That means an outdoorsman gets more warmth out of less fabric. Also, wool continues to trap warmth even when soaking wet. In fact, wool does such a good job of wicking away moisture that thin wool shirts make ideal warm-weather wear, too. Moreover, wool is a natural odor killer, keeping a kayak angler smelling fresh even after a day of hard paddling. Even though many synthetic materials are treated to kill odor-causing bacteria, wool's stink-fighting qualities are naturally built into the fibers. Not only that, but wool doesn't mean dry cleaning anymore. Most next-generation wool garments are washing-machine-safe as long as you lay them flat to dry. Be sure to look for wool materials that are chlorine-free and environmentally friendly, too.

Clothing companies looking for high-performance warmth are also returning to another natural fabric—goose down. Bird feathers have gotten some of the world's greatest explorers to some of the world's coldest places; most likely they'll take you wherever you want to go, too. But this isn't the poofy down that was in your dad's hunting vest. Patagonia has a line of down sweaters designed to be worn as outerwear or as an inner layer under a hard shell. The amazing thing about down is that it is a highly lofty material. That means that its poofiness traps warmth. Even more amazing is how that loft can be compressed—the whole sweater can be compacted to fit in your pocket. If feather down is warm enough for a goose sitting on a half-frozen lake, then it's certainly warm enough for the kayak angler sitting next to him.

Ironically, too much clothing can actually make you colder. Not only will 14 layers of clothes become clammy and dank, but they will crimp your style as well. Cold can be exacerbated by poor circulation, and a fisherman, especially, needs to maintain mobility. I've seen guys knock things overboard, bumble with their equipment, even injure themselves because they were overdressed.

When the cold is brutal, I add another layer—a breathable soft shell that insulates while stopping the wind. This layer is also water-resistant and can double as an outer layer in spring and fall. Try to find a shell that doesn't have too many pockets and attachments that would keep it from fitting under a dry top or rain jacket.

All of the above-mentioned clothes fit under a pair of 5-millimeter Hodgman waders and an Aquaskinz dry top, leaving me dry and toasty—and (relatively) safe. Anglers fishing in extremely cold or extremely wet conditions would want to add a layer of Mysterioso long johns under the pants, and wear a dry suit. Any colder than that and you'll need an Inuit *annuraaq*.

HOT-WEATHER OUTFITTING

Sure, it's important to dress properly for the cold, but what about the heat? When it comes to dressing for summer, less is less, right? A pair of Speedos and a fishnet tank top will keep a kayak angler cool even on the hottest day. Right?

Wrong. Many people think that the less clothing they wear, the cooler they will be. That's not exactly right. When dressing for the cold, less is more; when dressing for the heat, more is more. In summer I used to run around barefoot, barebacked, and sunburned. Then my wife noticed a mole on my back that was taking on a life of its own. A couple of months and half a dozen doctor's visits later I went under the knife to have a melanoma and lymph node removed. Now my skin never sees the light of day. I'm covered from head to toe—even on the hottest days of summer—and any exposed skin gets a thick lather of SPF 45.

When the temperature hits 90 with matching humidity, I'm dressed in long pants, shoes, long-sleeved shirt, and a hat. What I've discovered is that I'm actually cooler when I'm protected from the sun than I would be fully exposed. With the proper fabrics covering my body, it's as if I'm sitting in the shade everywhere I go. Moreover, the polyester fabrics that pull moisture away from my skin in winter perform the same function in summer. In the heat, however, these loose fabrics pull the perspiration away from my skin and move it to the outside of the fabric, where it dries quickly. The process works like a mini air conditioner keeping me cool and dry. When putting together your "summer look," get fabrics that dry quickly.

Perspiration and moisture shouldn't blotch in spots on the shirt or pants; they should be spread out by the fabrics so the moisture can dry more quickly.

Your shirt and pants must wick moisture, and they must protect you from the sun as well—not only to reduce your risk of nasty maladies like skin cancer and sunburn, but also to keep you cool. Many fabrics are rated for UV protection, which is fine, but super fabrics like those made by Mysterioso are tested to determine their SPF— sun protection factor. These high-tech materials are constructed with flatlock stitching for the greatest level of sun protection. Add a sun hat, thin gloves, and even a bandanna around your face, and you'll be completely covered.

Most fishing shirts tout a UPF rating—ultraviolet protection factor. Whether SPF or UPF, the number following the acronym indicates how long you can stay in the sun before your skin begins to suffer damage. For instance, the sun will begin to burn exposed skin in about five minutes. A typical white cotton T-shirt would have an SPF of about 5, which means you could gets five times the protection—or 25 minutes—by wearing a simple white shirt. SPF sunscreen with a rating of 15 would provide about 75 minutes of protection, while clothes and lotions that sport a rating of 45 or higher offer a whole day's worth of sun shade.

However, sunscreens with a SPF of 45 will not last all day. Sweat and water will quickly break the lotion down. To stay protected, reapply sunscreen every hour or so. Now, not all sunscreens with an SPF of 45 are created equal. I look for something without any fragrance—which is hard to find. I also like a lotion that isn't greasy. I've settled on Bull Frog and Neutrogena lotions, but there are a host of other specialty sunscreens designed for sportsmen—try to pick one that spreads easily, doesn't wash off, and smells good.

Kayak anglers are especially susceptible to sunburn. To begin with, we're floating around in a plastic boat without any shade. On top of that, we're sitting on water that reflects the sun's rays up into our face. To make matters worse, sitting in a kayak exposes the tender underside of our legs—an area that rarely sees the sun. I've had friends return from their first kayak trip unable to sit down because of their burned thighs. One buddy had to go to the hospital for third-degree burns that made his sunburned legs boil and blister. Terrible.

Simply applying sunscreen can help prevent sunburn and cancer—and even keep you cool. Since I went militant with the sun protection, I've noticed that I'm not as hot on the water. Obviously, being burned to a crisp makes your skin feel hot. Everyone who has spent any time outside is familiar with that skin-on-fire sensation. It also seems that a sunburn makes me tired. Of course, after a long day in the sun, I'm usually tired anyway, but I seem to be able to go longer and farther when I'm not sizzling like bacon left too long in the pan. The best argument for total sun protection, though, is the pain. Sunburn pain can be excruciating.

The last element in the equation is a good pair of wading shoes. Many anglers go Fred Flintstone in the kayak, preferring to leave their shoes in the trunk of their car when they go out for a summer 'yak stroll. The problem is, you'll definitely run into sun and most likely run into sharp objects while out on the water. I don't like to take a chance with either. Nothing is more painful than sunburned feet. It's hard to walk and impossible to wear shoes—I've even become physically sick from sunburned feet. Unfortunately, suntan lotion doesn't last long on your toes. Also, I always seem to be running into oyster bars, barnacle-encrusted pilings, and other sharp things on the water. To keep myself protected, I wear a pair of Bite Primal sneakers. These shoes have a rubber anti-slip sole that keeps my feet firmly planted on a rolling boat deck; their mesh body keeps my feet protected while allowing the water to flow in and out as I wade. I feel more confident and comfortable in a good pair of wading shoes than I would if I was constantly worrying about injuring my feet.

With all the clothes and accessories available to a kayak angler today, there is no reason to stop fishing because of the weather. I've fished on 100-degree days, in 90 percent humidity, through snowstorms, thunderstorms, even hurricanes. I've fished with ice on my kayak and with sweat rolling down my face. When you've only got one weekend—two precious days, 48 short hours—each week to pursue your passion, you've gotta go regardless of the weather. Modern fabrics and time-tested clothing systems make this possible. Neither snow, nor rain, nor heat, nor gloom of night need keep a kayak angler off the water.

Spring and fall, an angler can get away with a pair of breathable waders and sun-resistant shirt.

Kayak Maintenance

One of the biggest advantages to kayak fishing is the lack of maintenance a kayak requires. Caring for a motorboat requires hours of tinkering, lubing, fixing, adjusting, greasing, cleaning, outfitting, and refitting. A kayak needs but a few minutes. After most trips, I simply unload my 'yak from the roof of my jeep, hit it quick with the hose to knock off the fish slime and swamp mud, tip it over to let the water drain out . . . and then forget about it. If it's winter and I'm wearing my waders, I'll spray them off and hang them to dry. Once they're dry on the outside, I store them inside out to keep the toes from accumulating water. In the same sweep, I hit my electronics, paddle, reels and rods, and any tackle that I've used with the hose. I follow the tackle spray-down with a healthy dose of WD-40 and lay the stuff out on towels to dry. I'll then spray down my jeep to get any salt off and roll away the hose.

Every couple of months (and sometimes longer) I break out a sponge and a bottle of Soft Scrub and give the 'yak a thorough cleaning. The cleanser will scrub away the deep dirt and make the 'yak look like new.

Kayaks are very user-friendly. In fact, they take incredible abuse and give dependable service. I drag my kayak across parking lots, down beaches, and up and down launch ramps without a second thought. I've dropped it from the roof of my car and even crushed it under my tires. I store my kayak in my driveway and have plenty of room left over for two SUVs. I can drive around town for a week or more without ever taking my 'yak off the jeep roof.

In my neck of the woods, when the striped bass are running, I can get the call to hit the beach at any minute. I've gotten the call to chase down diving birds and blitzing fish in the middle of lunch, while driving to the grocery store, and out of a dead sleep. No time to load—just go! Jump in the jeep and head to the oceanfront. Other times I'm on my way from point A to point B, minding my own business, when I suddenly get the urge to check the ocean for action. So I pull up to the boardwalk—a ghost town in the middle of January—and see gannets swirling and diving on fish breaking just off the beach. A few phone calls later, my crew is jumping into action. SUVs converge on the spot and, in short order, we're all pushing through the shore break and paddling like hell. It's like an episode of the *Super Friends* cartoon.

Okay, so kayak fishing probably won't make you into a super-hero. It can make you into a better person, though. Really. If you're messy, you'll have to get organized. If you're a pack rat, you'll have to cut the fat. If you're mechanically inept, you'll have to learn to drill, screw, drive, and rivet. Kayaking gets you up off the couch and out on the water. If some problem of terrestrial life is bothering you, a few hours in a 'yak can often put it into perspective. If you have an addiction, you can turn it into a passion for kayak fishing. I've met most of my friends through kayak fishing; some of my friends, I've turned on to kayak fishing.

But it's not just the fishing. Many times I go out on the water to kayak more than to fish. And there's nothing like a long-distance paddle for some quality soul searching and self-reflection. In fact, much of this book was conceived on the water. Like I said, 'yak fishing really can make you a better person.

5

Paddling for Fish

Whether you're gliding through a mat of lily pads in search of bucketmouth bass, or breaking through the surf to chase down a knot of blitzing stripers, or winding through barnacle-encrusted bridge pilings looking for snook, half the fun of kayak fishing is the kayaking. Armed with only a paddle and bobbing on a plastic boat, it's exhilarating to face the wildest whims of Mother Nature. Peeling through choppy seas, sliding through glass-calm backwaters, surfing down breaking waves, running a standing rip, being carried by a raging river—kayaking is fun.

It's pretty easy, too. Neophyte kayak anglers can climb on a kayak, paddle a considerable distance, and catch a fish on their first day in the stirrups. Nothing to it. My wife outfished me on her first kayak fishing trip . . . and for that matter her second one. My brother, who is more accustomed to running a 60-foot headboat, can operate a kayak and catch fish. I've got a kayak colleague who is a septuagenarian and regularly surf launches to chase down big striped bass. Even my mother-in-law loves to kayak fish.

In fact, kayak fishing is so easy, it's dangerous. Sit-on-top boats, which are stable, maneuverable, and nearly indestructible, give inexperienced kayakers a deceptive sense of safety. Overestimate your abilities and the capabilities of your kayak and you could end up in big trouble. The more time I spend in my kayak, the more I realize its limitations and my liabilities.

When I first started kayak fishing, I liked to extend open invitations to anyone hungry enough to join me on one of my epic outings: paddling 5 miles out, spending 15 hours on the water, covering 12 miles in a day, and fishing for sea monsters. Guys would show up at the launch in all manner of kayaks. They would often fill their boats with every piece of fishing gear they owned and a bunch of stuff they'd borrowed from their buddies. Rarely would they bring a lunch—or even bottled water. Often they were wearing only a pair of swim trunks and an old T-shirt—no rain gear, no sun protection, no hat. Of course, no electronics—they wouldn't even carry a VHF radio. But what they lacked in equipment they made up for in enthusiasm. These guys were dangerous. I took 'em anyway. I was looking for company, and company was hard to find. Plus, I didn't want to seem elitist. I couldn't bring myself to tell someone, "You can't go because you suck."

Yet I wasn't doing these guys or myself any favors. They would inevitably lag behind. Expend all of their energy making the paddle. Suffer the whole day. Then catch nothing. In the end they would wish they had never gone fishing, never bought a kayak, and never met me.

I was lucky. The worst that ever happened was a bad sunburn one time, a hungry angler another, and a bad case of seasickness. Amazingly, all these guys made it back to the landing alive. In fact, knock on wood, to my knowledge we have yet to lose a kayak angler. Which only proves how easy and safe kayak fishing is—because there have certainly been times when we *should* have lost a guy or two. But don't be deceived. Just because you bought a kayak and all the bells and whistles, don't push the limit of your abilities and equipment. Just because it's easy to jump in a kayak and paddle away, don't neglect to take that paddling course. Just because nothing bad has happened yet doesn't mean it won't. Be careful out there.

Paddling Technique

The only instruction I've ever received on paddling was on my first day in a kayak. My buddy Kevin Whitley, who already had a few years' paddling experience under his belt (including a kayak tour from Georgia to Virginia), showed me how to make a proper paddle stroke, repeating instructions he'd gotten from a book.

Kevin had me place my hands on the paddle shaft shoulder width apart. He told me to imagine that I was looking at my reflection in a mirror. "Now," he said, "imagine that you're punching that reflection in the chin." With every downstroke, I'd bring my top hand across the kayak at chin level. Then Kevin expertly turned his kayak and paddled away from me. That was it. Lesson over.

That first night, and many subsequent nights, I followed Kevin's instructions but could not follow Kevin. My technique was weak. On every downstroke I'd bang the paddle into the side of the kayak. Scrape my knuckles on the hull. Dip the paddle blade too deep or not deep enough. Soon my back would be throbbing, my arms rubber, my butt screaming in pain. *Yeah, this is fun*, I thought.

But I kept punching my reflection in the mirror. And my stroke kept getting stronger, and my paddling became more comfortable, and I stopped banging my knuckles into the kayak, and I went faster and farther. Before I knew it I was paddling like a pro.

Now my paddle blades are an extension of my arms. I've noticed that I no longer whack the boat with my hands. My blade enters the water at the same angle and the same depth every time. I paddle with my hands lower, putting the shaft of the paddle apex between my knees on each stroke. I don't think about paddling; often I make adjustments without even realizing that I'm doing so. Like walking down the street, I don't think about every step; I just point myself in the right direction and go.

The Right Moves

Beyond the basic go-forward paddle stroke, there are a few fancy maneuvers that a kayak angler will want to master. Fish move through the water effortlessly, kayaks . . . less so. To keep up with your quarry, try to paddle like a fish.

SOFT TURN

To adjust the direction your kayak is traveling, take an extra stroke on the side of the boat opposite the direction you want to turn toward.

ABRUPT TURN

To make an abrupt turn, reach forward and dig the paddle into the water on the opposite side from the direction you wish to turn.

Pull hard with your low hand while pushing with the opposite hand.

HARD TURN

To make a hard turn to the starboard or port, reverse the paddle blade so that it's facing forward; dig it in on the side you want the boat to turn, then push forward.

Suicide Turn

When I'm fishing tight to structure—say, paddling between the pilings under a bridge—I'll use this stroke to pivot myself around one of the supports.

While you're going forward at a good clip, suddenly reach forward and dig your paddle into the water at a 45-degree angle to the boat. Be careful: This move will either snap the kayak around or catapult you into the drink.

Reverse

The quickest way to go into reverse or stop the boat is to spin the kayak paddle in your hand until the blade faces are pointing forward.

Then lean back in the seat and dig one blade into the water.

Starting at the kayak hull, push forward while twisting your body.

Repeat on the opposite side.

SLOW REVERSE

A slower way to go into reverse or reduce your speed is to perform the same maneuver as above—but without spinning the paddle blade. Instead, dig the spine of the paddle into the water.

ONE-EIGHTY

To turn the kayak 180 degrees, combine the hard turn with the reverse strokes.

Start by spinning the paddle so the face of the blades is pointing forward. Then dig in at the rear of the kayak and push forward.

Continue this stroke on the side you want to turn toward until the boat has turned 90 degrees.

Spin your paddle again so that the blade is facing the back of the boat. Now make forward strokes on the opposite side of the kayak.

Combine forward and back strokes until the kayak comes around 180 degrees.

SIDE SLIDE

Sometimes you have to move sideways.

Start with the paddle extended and the blade parallel with the kayak.

Pull the blade toward you while feathering it from side to side in an S-pattern through the water. This keeps the blade from spinning the boat instead of moving it sideways across the water.

Turn the blade perpendicular to the boat and push it away from you to start the next stroke.

ONE-HANDED PADDLING

Many times—especially in the heat of battle with a big fish—you have to work your tackle and your kayak at the same time. It pays to learn how to paddle with one hand, then practice the technique for just such occasions.

To paddle on one side, brace the shaft of the paddle with your forearm and use your whole shoulder to push the blade through the water.

To paddle on the other side, use your chest as a fulcrum and pull the blade with your free hand.

Maneuvering

Kayak fishing definitely takes a little more paddling than just kay-aking. You'll need to maneuver the craft within range of the fish: holding your boat over structure, chasing down moving fish, and sneaking up on hiding fish.

And yet we can't paddle and work a fishing rod simultaneously. Both actions take two hands and, unfortunately, we are only given enough appendages to perform one act at one time. Guys pedaling Hobie kayaks, which use a pedal-and-fin propulsion system, have an advantage in this area, but are at a loss in others. Hobie operators may be able to cast, reel, and jig while pedaling, turning, or holding their kayaks in the current, but they can't go backward, go sideways, or spin on their axis without using a paddle.

When a big fish hits, pandemonium breaks loose as the angler attempts to clear the other lines while holding on to the bowed-up rod with all his might. The best policy is to forget about the other lines and concentrate on the fish. Many trophies are lost when the angler gets distracted from the prime directive.

For traditional kayakers, maneuvering your boat to target fish takes some skill and a lot of practice. The more you do it, the better you get. And a master kayaker, with total control over the craft, can be lethal on the fish.

In fact, one of the advantages of a kayak is that we can take our plastic boats places that other boaters wouldn't dare to venture. No, we can't go as far as motorboaters, but we can get a lot closer to the fish.

Proper paddle position. To keep the paddle secure and out of the way, lay it across your lap so that it's parallel to the kayak.

Fishing On and Near Structure

Fish love structure, and so do fishermen. The closer you can get to rocks, the closer you can get to fish. When I'm fishing a jetty, I'll maneuver my kayak right into the rocks, letting the boulders scrape my plastic while I hold my rod over the opposite side to bounce a jig around the base of the jetty. Nothing is better than pulling fat flounder out of the rocks before an audience of boaters who aren't catching anything.

It is no secret that bridges, jetties, and breakwaters hold fish. A kayak can get close to the structure to get close to the biggest fish.

One of my favorite places to fish is the jetty at the mouth of Little Creek Inlet in Norfolk, Virginia. Almost every fish that swims the Chesapeake can be found at the tip of this jetty. My buddies and I often hit this spot after work, just before dark, and from spring through fall we pull flounder and reds over 20 inches, croaker up to 18, chopper blues in the 30-inch range, and good-sized speckled

trout from the structure, all under the glaring eyes of gawking
boaters. One time I heard a boater tell his buddy, "Damn, those
kayakers are kicking our ass." In fact, one of the guys who fished the
area regularly in his $30,000 center console has since bought a kayak
and joined us.

But that doesn't mean fishing around rocks, pilings, and walls is
a walk in the park. It's tough.

First, there are many dangers close to structure. Even though a
kayak can be ground into barnacles and concrete without busting a
leak—the sides and the bottom of my boat look like raw ham-
burger—fishing around hard surfaces has its dangers. First, pushing
off concrete with your hands or feet can tear up your skin. Also,
taking a direct hit from a bridge piling can dislocate an arm or
shoulder. One night I was paddling below a bridge when a big wave
lifted my kayak. On my upstroke, I hit the blade on one of the bridge
supports with the full force of my arm. Whack! I thought I had torn
my arm out of its socket. After "walking it off," though, I was able to
continue along the bridge and return to shore.

One of the worst scenarios is one of the most unexpected for
new kayak anglers. Let's say you're fishing along a jetty or in an area
with submerged stumps or pilings. Of course the negligible draft of
a kayak allows you to pass over the stumps or hover over the jetty
rocks and get close to the fish. But suppose a wave comes along. The
water rises with the wave, lifting your kayak, then recedes, dropping
you onto the structure. Now you're no longer sitting on the water,
you're sitting on a rock or log. Even worse, the kayak is no longer
being supported by the water; it's teetering on a solid surface. That's
bad. Not only will you most likely fall out, but you could strike other
solid surfaces on your descent. Ouch.

Kayak anglers have to be super sensitive to their surroundings.
I've had big boats suck the water out from under me before they
even passed. I've been tossed by a boat wake into the rocks from what
I thought was a safe distance. One time a ship passing through a pair
of jetties displaced so much water, it created a whirlpool big enough
to suck me and my kayak to the bottom.

Don't be afraid to throw your body into your kayaking. Legs make effective stabilizers, rudders, and brakes. To stop, turn, and cast on a school of breaking fish, drop your leg into the water and fire off a shot.

The trick to fishing structure is getting a feel for the water running past it. Rocks, trees, and pilings are usually stationary, while water is not—and it's very tricky to remain stationary in your kayak while sitting atop a liquid that is constantly moving in weird and unpredictable ways. Motorboats are too big and heavy to be effective at this. Kayaks, on the other hand, are light and sensitive. You can detect the slightest shift in the current and adjust your position.

Isaac Newton said, "An object in motion tends to stay in motion . . . unless acted upon by an unbalanced force." That guy must have been a kayaker. Once you get your kayak in motion, it will stay in motion unless you change direction or the water under the boat changes direction or velocity. This means you can propel the kayak forward with the paddle, and it will continue on that course until the passing water stops it. Because the kayak still carries momentum, however, even after it stops, it will hold in the current until its forward energy is expended and the current begins to push it back in the opposite direction.

In other words, always try to fish structure with the bow of your 'yak facing into the current or wind. On a good day, the current and wind will work against each other to hold you in one spot. On a bad day, current and wind will work together to push you away from the fish. Since a kayak is designed to track through the water in a straight line, it will hold in the current in a straight line (like a bicycle in a track stand) until you or the water changes direction. This takes a lot of practice—but once you've mastered it, it can really improve your fishing.

Current works in weird ways around structure, too. I've fished places where the tide was coming in but the current was still moving out. Crazy eddies spin and boil around structure, and these can either help you hover over the fish or frustrate all your efforts to stay still. You'll often find dead spots around structure where you can hide while casting into current running nearby.

This is a great reason to kayak fish: You can get right into the places where fish live, taking the fight to them.

Pilings

Our apparently insatiable desire for progress has done little good for fish. Building suburbs produces sewage, farming causes runoff, dredging alters habitat, and paving roads diverts stormwater into fishing water. But building bridges may be one of the best things we've ever done for fish—and fishermen. It is no secret that bridge pilings, pier pilings, oil rig legs, and dock pilings hold bass, stripers, trout, panfish, reds, snook, and sheepshead. Fish love the safety and seclusion they find in this structure.

It is also no secret that kayak anglers have an advantage when it comes to fishing such fish-holding structure. We can get closer while being quieter and put the bait right into the strike zone.

Pilings don't just offer fish a great refuge; they provide the same service to kayak fishermen. In pumping wind and cranking current—even rain—pilings are a welcome shelter against the storm. I've spent hours hiding behind pilings while the current screamed and the wind howled around me.

There are six sides to each piling. Now, before the engineers out there protest, remember that when we fish a piling, we aren't fishing the actual piling but rather the water that runs around it. Water moving with the current flows past a piling in six different places: front, front right and left, rear right and left, and the back of the piling.

First, the front. As the current approaches the piling, it will pile up on the front of the pole. Fish love to station themselves here, facing into the current, waiting for a passing morsel. But the fish aren't always right in front of the piling. In fact, you'll often find fish several feet off the front, taking advantage of the rushing water piling up behind them.

Motorboaters target these fish by moving slowly along the uptide side of the structure, holding the boat a cast away from the pilings and tossing lures. Kayakers have a hard time with this. Most of the time, we cannot maneuver and fish at the same time. We have to keep our bow into the current, which means we're facing away from the piling. Under light current conditions or the unusual occasion when wind and current are cooperating, we can turn our stern into the current and combine backpaddling with casting. But that rarely happens. To target fish holding in front of the piling, pull your kayak directly in front of bridge and let the current push you into the piling; you, meanwhile, are using one hand to hold your craft off the barnacles (another reason to wear gloves) and the other to dangle a bait in front of the critters hovering below.

This maneuver is especially productive at night under a lighted bridge. Look at the shadow created by the lights falling from above. You'll often see fish hovering with their noses on the line, waiting for your swim bait or plug to pass in front.

Fish are weird. I've never figured out what it is that they like about swimming in front of a piling. Seems to me like this would be the worst place to be with a running current. Still, it's easy to figure out why they hang out along other places on the piling—protection. That's why kayakers hang around pilings, too. There are five protected places on the piling. As the current approaches and rushes into the front, it swirls along the side and passes out the back of the bridge, pier, or tower. A baitfish caught in the current will also swirl past the piling.

To imitate this helpless bait, paddle your kayak 5 to 10 feet from the side of the piling, lob a swim bait or plug into the front corner, and let it drift past while taking up slack with the reel. One of the hardest kayaking skills to master is stopping. That's right—it is hard to stop a kayak. But I'm not talking about arresting progress; I'm talking about timing your stop to keep from gliding across fish or into the structure.

As you approach a piling, you're performing a complex physics equation in your head to figure out how fast you have to go forward in order to glide to a stop without overshooting the target. A perfect approach will give you three opportunities to cast on a piling. As you paddle toward it, with the kayak still moving forward, you can fire one cast off and retrieve. Then, as the kayak pauses in the current before being swept backward, fire and retrieve another cast. Finally, the kayak will succumb to the forces of nature and start to drift away from the piling. Fire off another cast and retrieve. If three casts haven't produced one fish, move on to another piling and start the process again.

Without a doubt, the best place to find fish on a piling is in the current eddy behind the structure. Not only is it a good place to find fish, it's also a good place *to* fish. Because a kayak is light and stream-lined, it can hover in the dead space behind a piling for a surprising length of time.

Obviously, one way to target fish hiding in the lee of a piling is to pull up to the structure, drop bait to the bottom, and jig it up and down or work it to the surface. I've spent stretches of better than six hours holding my kayak behind a huge piling on the Chesapeake Bay Bridge Tunnel, dangling a live eel off the bottom as water rushed past me like a raging river.

Many times, however, the fish aren't right behind the piling. You'll find them much farther back, holding in the turbulent, con-fused water mixing well in back of the structure. To target these fish,

I pull behind one piling, station myself in the eddy, and cast to the next nearest piling. The bait will sweep in the current into the mouths of fish hanging behind the piling.

When I hook a fish behind a piling, total pandemonium ensues. The same structure that was just my best friend becomes my enemy as it aids my adversary in his attempts to escape. That's when the fun starts. Of course, the key is to keep the fish out of the structure. Paddle with one hand, pass the rod to the outside of the boat, and kick off the piling with your feet—or push off with your hands—until you can get clear. With big fish, though, that can be a problem; you may have to follow your catch through the structure. I've had 40-pound striped bass pull me through barnacle-encrusted concrete and we've both survived. Try to keep the line as short as possible, stay over the fish, use your legs, arms, and shoulders to body-check the concrete, and fight the fish with your fingers crossed. Only in a kayak!

Bridge pilings are probably one of the places you'll most consistently find fish. Whether fresh water or salt, if you're new to an area—find a bridge and you'll most likely find big predator fish. Screaming current and rioting water merely serve to break up schools of bait and tear down the little guys' only defense—strength in numbers. The alpha species we target love adverse conditions—and so should we.

Anchoring

Anchoring is one of the most dangerous activities you can perform in a kayak. Most of my close calls have come while trying to anchor my boat in wind, waves, and current. Tethering a light plastic boat on the open water is an opportunity for disaster. Even with an anchor trolley system (see chapter 4), getting the anchor from the kayak to the end of the trolley takes a lot of skill and a little luck. Honing anchoring skills takes planning and practice—or you're sure to take a swim.

Start with plenty of rope—three times the water depth. This accomplishes two things: First, it takes a rope of at least one and a half times to the water depth to anchor. So if you're anchoring in 20 feet of water—you'll need 30 feet of rope. Add wind and current and you'll need even more.

This angler is anchored with his rope running off his bow trolley. Notice how another line runs to the stern with a carabiner in between. Also, note the pool noodle foam that serves as a buoy on his anchor line.

Second, extra rope translates into extra time to set the anchor and safely get your kayak situated. Anchoring becomes dangerous when the rope comes tight and your boat is side-to the current and wind. It flips, you go for a dip, end of story. With extra rope, you get extra time. Once the anchor is in the bottom and the boat is situated, you can always retract line to move over structure.

Careful planning and practice—even performing anchoring drills on calm days in protected waters—can prevent tragedy. If you're fishing over sandy bottom, start with a Bruce or Danforth anchor; over rocks or windfalls, use a collapsing grapple anchor. If you're fishing in deep water—more than 50 feet—add a 3- to 5-foot length of chain to ensure that it sticks. Use a bowline knot to tie an appropriate length of 5-millimeter nylon rope to the anchor. Be sure to choose a high-quality anchor rope that won't get hopelessly tangled or knotted. Heavier rope with less memory is much more user-friendly than the thin, wimpy stuff.

To keep from losing the anchor should you lose hold of the rope, slide a big crab pot buoy over the rope and down to the anchor. When I arrive on the scene, I first check that the anchor rope, anchor, and buoy are clear and free of tangles and snags. I slide anchor and buoy over the side and feed out line until the anchor hits the bottom. I continue to feed out line until I have enough rope out to equal one and a half times the water depth. Then I tie an overhand loop in the line to catch the buoy.

Now the tricky stuff starts. As my kayak continues to drift back in the current, I quickly and carefully snap the line in the anchor trolley clip. With the line still paying out of the cockpit, passing through the clip, I pull the trolley line to run the carabiner to the bow or stern. Only then do I tie off the line on a cleat, squeeze it into a cam, or loop it around a grommet in my boat. Whichever system you choose to secure the anchor line in your boat, be sure the line can quickly be untied and released in case of an emergency. Whether you're freeing the anchor line to fight a fish or to avoid impending waves or an inbound boat, simply loosen the rope and let it pass through the trolley clip with the buoy keeping it afloat. After the coast is clear, you can return to recover the buoy, rope, and anchor.

Pulling the anchor is just as dangerous as setting it. Your best option is to release the anchor, then paddle back upcurrent. Once you've recovered the buoy and pulled the rope tight over the anchor, yank like hell until it comes loose. Be sure to keep the line clear in the cockpit, and the buoy attached. If you can't free the anchor before the current catches your kayak and pushes it back, let go of the rope, resituate yourself, and return to give it another try. If that doesn't work, you can run the anchor rope down the stern anchor trolley, secure it to the boat, and paddle hard against the current in the direction opposite the anchor.

Note that while this is effective in a motorboat with hundreds of horses pulling on the anchor, it hardly ever works in a kayak powered by a couple of pythons. You may well have to abandon the anchor and return to try again when the current has subsided or your energy has returned. Sometimes you won't get your anchor back. Whatever you do, don't let the anchor pull you into the water—then the anchor wins and you lose.

Stand and Maneuver

When sight fishing, a kayak angler will get a better view of the water by standing in his boat.

Start with one hand on the end of the paddle blade and the other midway down the shaft.

Then, to switch sides with the paddle, cross your arms,

And reverse hand positions.

Surf Launching

If anchoring is one of the most dangerous kayak fishing maneuvers, launching and recovering through the surf is *the* most dangerous. Even the best kayaks are in serious danger in the surf. Nothing will flip a 'yak faster than a wave to the gunnel. Breaking surf is unpredictable and powerful beyond belief, and there's nowhere to hide if events turn ugly. Things happen fast in the surf—bad things.

I've spent a lot of my life playing in the surf: first on my dad's shoulder, then on the deck of a surfboard, and now in the cockpit of a kayak. Most of that time I was scared to death. Hey, nothing produces adrenaline like all-consuming terror—it's fun.

Losing or damaging expensive tackle and electronics is no joke, though. I can get wet and sandy and pummeled by the waves, but don't let me damage any rods, reels, or tackle! Unfortunately, a wipeout in the surf usually means an unplanned shopping trip to the local tackle store.

Before launching through the waves, be sure everything in your kayak is secured. I bungee my Crate Mate shut and run another bungee over my tacklebox. Don't forget to tie the anchor to the boat

All surf launches should be this easy. The key to a successful surf launch is starting with calm conditions.

so that it doesn't fall out—it might stick in the bottom and hold the kayak in the impact zone. If the surf isn't too rough, I'll leash my rods to the kayak. If it looks nasty, I'll store them in the bow hatch. If the waves are big and mean—I'll go home. With a manageable surf, I'll then load my stuff and drag my boat to the shore. Once everything is tied down and stowed away, I turn my attention to making it through the breaking waves and reaching the safety waiting on the other side of the surf zone.

To start, I stand on the shore, at the edge of the beach, watching the waves break while looking for a deep slough cutting through the shallow bar. A wave will break in water one and a half times as deep as the wave is high. So a 3-foot wave will break in 4½ feet of water. When looking for a way through the surf, look for water that is deeper than the above equation. Waves also come in sets of 3 to 10 breakers. I time the waves as they roll in, waiting for a pause in the sets. Once I identify a cut that will give me safer passage and wait until the last set of waves passes, I wade out as far as possible, holding the kayak by its bow handle with one hand and my paddle with the other. When I'm just past the shorebreak, in waist-deep to knee-deep water, I sit down in the kayak and start paddling like hell. The keys are to keep the bow facing into the waves and to maintain forward momentum. Be sure the scupper plugs are out of the kayak so water can drain out of the cockpit and through the tank well. If possible, aim for the shoulders of the waves, on either side of the peak, where the wave will break last. Whatever you do, don't stop paddling until you're far outside the breakers.

Launching may be exhilarating, but landing is nerve racking. At least when you're heading out, you can see the waves, maneuver to get around them, and paddle hard to get over them. On the way in you can't do any of that. You want to paddle like a man possessed to get out. To make it back to the beach, you have to slow it down and carefully time your way through the surf. The key is to handle your boat without giving control to the wave. First, identify the impact zone, where most of the waves are breaking, and stay behind the waves. When you detect a lull in the action, paddle hard to get through the zone between breakers. The safest place in the surf is right behind a breaking wave. Stay there as long as possible.

If you should get caught by a wave, try to keep your boat facing forward and let the wave push you to shore. Lean back to keep the bow elevated, and use your paddle to steer the boat straight. This is when a kayak with a pronounced rocker in its hull will be at an advantage.

If you find yourself sideways on the wave, lean into the breaking water to keep the surf from pushing you over. Lean back and push the flat edge of the paddle into the base of the wave to lean even farther in. Just try to keep the wave from rolling you.

Regardless of your best efforts to negotiate your way through the surf, thousands of tons of speeding water can be very unreasonable—mess around with breaking waves long enough and they will eventually mess you up. What then?

Well, if you're lucky, it will be shallow enough to stand up. In that case salvage whatever tackle is floating around you, grab the paddle, and, if it's not too rough, remount the kayak and paddle or waddle back to shore with what remains of your gear and your dignity.

If you're unlucky and it's too deep to paddle or wade back to shore, then you've got some problems. Of course you've got your PFD on, so drowning shouldn't be much of an issue. Go for the paddle. I've said this before, but it's worth repeating: It's easier to swim to the kayak carrying the paddle than it is to chase down the paddle while dragging the kayak. Be careful to keep the waves from turning your kayak into a weapon—stay between the breakers and the boat so that it doesn't roll over you or hit you in the head. Once you get on the inside the breakers, you should be able to remount your boat and limp to shore. Always remember the first rule of extreme sports: *Abandon gear to save life and limb.* Whatever your rods, reels, rigs, and tackle are worth, they're not worth your life.

One of the most humiliating wipeouts I ever suffered in my 'yak happened before I'd even gotten in. I was standing on the shore, holding the bow handle while watching the surf for an opportunity to launch. Next thing I knew I was lying on the ground, looking up at the sky, with the shore break rolling me around in the sand while

I listened to the laughter of my fishing buddy standing over me. What happened?

A wave had broken on shore. The water ran up the beach, lifting my boat. As the wave receded, it carried my kayak with it, which caught me in the back of the legs and knocked out my feet like a perfectly placed judo kick. Never underestimate the surf—it plays dirty.

Landing Fish

The one kayak fishing question I get more than any other is: "How do you land fish in that thing?" The answer I always give is: "Any way possible." Nothing will test your creativity as a kayak angler more than finally getting your catch into the boat. Each fish offers a different set of problems.

Landing a fish is also one of the best aspects of fishing from a kayak: It gets you face-to-face with a big nasty sea beast—so close

Landing toothy critters in a kayak should be accomplished with great care. Keep fingers away from the dangerous ends and try to control the fish in the cockpit.

you can smell his breath—then lets you wrestle him into your lap, sub-
duing the monster with your hands and legs. It's totally Neanderthal.

Of course, with smaller fish, a petite landing net works well. The
problem is, there's no good place to store a net on a kayak. The net
catches fish, all right, but it also seems to catch every handle, hook,
eye, grommet, and rod tip on the boat—especially when you need
it the most. Still, when you're dealing with spiny, toothy critters, a
net will help you stay uninjured. For other fish, you don't really need
a net.

My best fishing buddy, Kevin Whitley, has invented an almost
surefire way to land everything from big flounder to monster striped
bass and red drum. He calls it the Flounder Scoop. Here's how it
works. As the fish approaches the boat, grab the line or leader with
one hand and use it to direct the fish until he's parallel to the boat,
with his head facing toward the stern and his tail stretching to the

How do you land a big fish in a kayak? Any way you can.

Once on board, a big fish rides between the 'yaker's legs—be sure to exercise all proper caution.

bow. Dip your foot into the water and pull the fish atop your leg. Finally, in one quick movement, lift the fish with leg and leader and scoop it into the cockpit.

This method is harmless to both fish and angler. By lifting the fish's body with your wet leg, you support his organs out of the water and maintain his slime coat. Moreover, once the fish is in the

The scoop: To land a fish without a landing net, bring it headfirst alongside the boat, drop your foot into the water under the fish, then lift the leader and your leg to scoop the fish into the cockpit.

cockpit (if he doesn't have pointy appendages or sharp teeth), cover him with your legs to keep him from flopping out or injuring himself banging around.

To store fish on their way to the frying pan, use a stringer and dangle them in the water while the kayak is at rest, then carry them

A small net that floats helps make sure dinner ends up in the boat, not back in the water.

in your lap when you're under way. If you are paddling waters filled with dangerous sharks or hungry sea lions, a stringer may invite an unwelcome dinner guest. In this case, employ an insulated fish bag that will keep your catch cool while you're on the way back to the dock.

Dinner is served.

That's it. From buying your kayak, to rigging it out, arming it with tackle and gear, dressing for the conditions, planning for the worst-case scenario, picking a place to fish, handling the kayak, and landing the catch—you're now ready to fish out of a kayak. Go get 'em!

6

Regional Review

Even though the information covered in the preceding chapters applies to kayak fishing in fresh water, salt water, inshore, and offshore from the North to the South and East to West, there are many tips and tricks that are specific to one region or one type of kayak fishing. To obtain the latest, greatest local knowledge, I've tracked down some of the best anglers around the country. Here's what they had to say.

Southern California/Baja Mexico
Angler: Jim Sammons
Specialty: Yellowtail, white sea bass, dolphin, billfish
"Southern California offers some of the most diverse fishing," says kayak guide Jim Sammons. "You have to be ready for anything from yellowtail to calico bass." That means having a kayak that's adaptable to any situation, whether trolling spoons, working live baits, or jigging with light tackle.

It also means there are plenty of opportunities for new anglers to get into kayak fishing. "I jumped straight into going offshore,"

Sammons says, "but that might not be a good idea." He recommends anglers start fishing in the bays. "There is fantastic fishing in San Diego Bay," he points out. "You can have 100-fish days on spotted bay bass and sand bass without having to deal with the swells found in the ocean."

Such protected waters also make a good place to practice fishing out of a kayak. "With the repetition of catching a lot of fish out of the kayak, the angler learns to move in the boat," Sammons explains. Through experience, you learn techniques for dealing with fish, grow familiar with how your boat behaves, and refine your cockpit layout. Hooking, fighting, and landing fish become second nature.

"The really cool thing," Sammons says, "is that it doesn't take a lot of high-end equipment to get started." He suggests new 'yakers pick up a lightweight spinning outfit suitable for 6-pound test and a handful of ⅛- to ¾-ounce jigs with corresponding 2- to 3-inch plastic grub tails. Sammons points anglers to the deeper holes, drop-offs, eel grass, and channels that provide structure where these bottom-hugging fish can hide. "The biggest mistake I see," he says, "is guys overfishing their lures." He instructs his clients to drop their offering to the bottom and let it tumble naturally with the current. He also tells them to fish on the move: "Troll a Frenzy while moving from spot to spot and work a spinnerbait through the grass beds." The key to fishing these backwaters is current. "If you want to catch fish," Sammons says, "you've got to fish moving water."

Once the basics are established, Sammons recommends you move out into the open water in search of bigger prey. "Our big-fish fishery is live-bait-dependent," he says. "Having a good live bait system is huge." Whether you pick up a store-bought tank or make your own, the key to a good system is circulation. "Bubbles only serve to knock the slime coat off the fish and kill the bait." The tank should be large enough to hold half a dozen baits; also look for one that constantly exchanges the water. Moreover, in southern climes, the water in the bucket will quickly overheat unless it is constantly replaced by cool, fresh water. To catch mackerel for bait, Sammons uses a Sabiki rig and a stout rod. "Don't go too light on the tackle," he suggests; "you don't want to fight your bait." Playing around with the bait could result in losing or injuring the fish. "You want to really crank 'em in."

When they're not fishing live bait, Sammons and his colleagues are trolling spoons and plugs. He pushes kayak models that can troll effectively to easily cover long distances at a steady pace. "Use a faster, longer boat," he says, "and a carbon-fiber paddle." To rig for the big fish, he installs two Scotty rod holders behind his seat. These keep the reels higher off the water; they don't get as wet as they would in a flush mount.

Of course the best way to learn the ropes is to hire a guide. Pros might take you to their secret fishing holes and show you how to rig the killer baits, and they'll definitely keep you out of danger and recommend ways to avoid problems on the water. Sammons also suggests taking a paddling class to improve your stroke. "A better paddler," he concludes, "is a better fisherman."

Northern California
Angler: Allen Bushnell
Specialty: Salmon and halibut

"We rig up our boats pretty much the same as the guys in Southern California," Allen Bushnell says, "except we don't use live wells as often." Instead, 'yakers fishing off Monterey, Santa Cruz, and points north rely on bait buckets to keep their anchovies, sardines, and smelt fresh and kicking. "Plano bait buckets are popular," he says, "but they're a real drag." Yes, these buckets will hold a day's worth of bait, but they're not the most streamlined contraptions on earth. "Most guys are custom-building bait buckets by drilling holes in a 2- to 3-foot section of 3- to 4-inch PVC tubing and attaching pointed caps on each end," he says, "like a torpedo."

Another difference Allen points out: "In Northern California we troll with our rods in front of us." Because these northern anglers are slow-trolling with 2 to 3 pounds of lead, or drifting (locally known as mooching) with up to 12 ounces of weight, they can't put a rod in free spool and turn on the clicker. "We have to watch the rod tip and set the hook." To facilitate this, Bushnell mounts a RAM rod tube in front of his center console. "It gives me a place to put the rod when I catch a fish," he says. When you're installing the RAM Mount, he recommends placing a metal backing plate under the plastic to keep big halibut or salmon from ripping the rod holder out of your boat.

Bushnell is careful about his rod and reel choices. "For mooching you want a parabolic rod," he says: "a lighter blank that takes the bend along the arch of rod." The rod should be at least 7 feet long to allow the angler to reach around the bow when fighting a fish. "I use a Calstar 196 with a fast tip and a Penn Jigmaster 500 reel." He prefers the classic Penn because it's a time-tested reel that can easily be repaired and offers countless opportunities for customization. "Shimano Calcuttas and Abu 6500s are also popular choices," he notes.

To fill his tacklebox, Bushnell picks from a variety of swim baits, plugs, and spoons. "I'll take a bunch of Megabait leadhead jigs from 3 to 7 inches and 2 to 10 ounces." He also likes a Hair Raiser with a white head and white hair. Plugs are popular, and Bushnell gives the nod to Rapala divers. He also packs a variety of Krocodile spoons.

For bait fishing, he ties up two-hook stinger rigs on 20-pound-test fluorocarbon with a size 2 single hook up front and a size 1 treble in the back. "Tie up a bunch of rigs," Bushnell suggests, "with the stinger at different lengths to fit different-sized baits."

For beginning anglers, Bushnell recommends fishing reefs and sandy areas in Santa Cruz harbor and around Capitola Warf. Anglers who have put some water under their keel will want to hit the edges and bait balls off Moss Landing from April to August in search of salmon. The kelp beds off Del Monte Beach also hold a variety of fish and are kayak-friendly.

Central/Northern California
Angler: Ricky Mitchell
Specialty: Fly fishing salt and fresh water

"A kayak can get right over underwater rock walls and boulders," says kayak fly angler Ricky Mitchell. "It's really the best way to explore."

When fishing famed bass holes like Millerton Lake in central California, he likes to get deep into the structure and steep drops that the fish use to ambush unsuspecting baits.

When it comes to tackle, go heavy. "I kept breaking the tips on the 6-weight fly rods that I had," Mitchell admits. "Anything less than 8- or 9-weight and you're asking for trouble." He leans toward a rod with faster action, noting: "You don't want to make a lot of backcasts." For a reel he suggests "something with a large arbor and high-quality drag appropriate for fresh or salt water." A reel isn't just a place to store line; it should be a deadly fish-beating tool with a cork drag and plenty of torque. "Don't go cheap," Mitchell advises. "Cheap fly reels will freeze up, possibly costing a big fish."

He tells newcomers that it doesn't take an expert to fly fish out of a kayak. "Once you get your cast down," he explains, "you can lay your backcast only a few inches off the water." He has trained himself to cast sidearm so that his backcast avoids the rods that he stores behind him.

Sometimes Mitchell fly fishes without fly casting. "People underestimate the effectiveness of trolling," he explains. He'll pitch his bait about out behind his boat and set the rod in a holder. Then he paddles along, dragging the fly behind him. "I go paddle–paddle–pause," he says, "giving the fly life with the paddle."

To land a fish on the fly, Mitchell uses a unique technique. "Lifting the fish with the fly rod will result in broken tackle," he points out. To avoid this, when he gets a fish close to the kayak, he reaches the rod behind him. "I lean the rod across my back and over using my shoulder as a fulcrum." Then he pulls the reel with his right hand to lift the rod tip—"like a see-saw." With the net in his left hand, he reaches out and scoops up the fish.

Mitchell sets up his kayak with all his gear behind him. "I like a nice clean cockpit," he says, "nothing to get in the way." He has installed rod holders at a 45-degree angle on his milk crate so that he can clear them with his backcast.

For flies, Mitchell goes with Buggers, Clousers, Deceivers, spinner flies, and—in salt water—bigger mackerel and shad flies.

"Size selection is as important as fly selection." He suggests keeping a range of flies on hand: Buggers from size 12 to size 2, and mackerel patterns up to 4/0. When he goes to spinning tackle, Mitchell relies on Rat-L-Trap and Rapala plugs.

Mitchell especially loves his kayak for its versatility. With the same equipment, he can go from fresh water to salt without missing a beat.

Gulf Coast
Angler: Captain Flip Spencer, Team Ocean Kayak
Specialty: Flats fishing for red drum, spotted sea trout, and flounder

"I use nothing but lures," Captain Flip Spencer says, "and I catch more fish than the guys who are using bait." Modern lures are designed to act more like an injured baitfish than an injured baitfish does. Years of testing and refinement have led to artificial baits that are functional works of art—as effective at catching fishermen as catching fish. Not to mention that lures are easier to work with than live bait. It can take hours of fishing time to procure bait, keep it alive, and rig it up. Lures are happy in a tacklebox stuffed into a kayak crate. "Today's technology makes is so much easier to use lures."

Spencer continues, "If I had my choice of five lures to fish the Gulf Coast, I'd take a silver and a gold spoon, a black-and-silver Top Dog She Pup, a Spook Jr. in bone, and an assortment of jigheads and paddle tails." Early in the morning he throws the topwater stuff. "Use bigger lures in spring and summer," he suggests, "to weed out the smaller fish." Later in the day he switches to spoons and jigs. "In thigh-deep water," he says, "use a ¼- to ½-ounce spoon, and in waist-deep water switch up to a ¾-ounce spoon."

Flip rigs his soft plastics so that they are weedless using a 5/0 H&H flutter hook. He also likes screw-on jigheads: "They hold the bait better." His plastic selection is dominated by natural-colored tails in new penny, salt and pepper, and pumpkin with a chartreuse tail. "Let the jig do the work," Flip suggests, explaining that a slow and steady retrieve is more effective than a sporadic jerk. He will vary the

Big fish like thick structure—so do kayak anglers.

retrieve on each cast until he finds out what's working. Then he sticks with that technique until the bite stops.

For tackle, Flip likes a medium-light- to medium-action 7.5-foot soft-tipped rod with plenty of backbone. "To test a rod," he instructs, "quickly flick the rod left-to-right. You don't want to see a double bow; that means the rod is too flimsy." The perfect rod will have a light tip to lob a light lure and a heavy backbone to put the hurt on a heavy fish. The 7-foot-long rod has several advantages. First, Flip explains, it makes setting the hook easier. Anglers using short rods have to lift the rod over their head to get a better angle for setting the hook. With a longer rod, you can quickly set the hook while holding the rod at chest level. Moreover, the longer rod helps when fighting a fish, making it easier to work the fish around the bow of the kayak.

"If you want to catch reds in spring and summer," Spencer says, "find the oysters." All types of bait are attracted to oyster beds, and the reds come in to take advantage of the buffet. Of course, working birds are always a good sign of feeding fish, and a silent kayak can drift right into the fray. When he's working a grass bed, he looks for the sand holes between clumps of grass. Predators will hide in the grass waiting for a meal to fall into any clearing.

To find trout, he looks for slicks on the surface of the water. "Sea trout will regurgitate what they have in their stomach to attract bait-fish." Kind of like chum. According to Flip, a big slick is usually a school of smaller trout, while a small one may be a single large fish working alone. Cast to the outside edge of the slick to find the fish. "The slick will smell like cut grass or watermelon," he adds. Man, what are those trout eating?

Obviously, Flip spends a lot of time looking for fish. To see them, he likes to stand in his kayak. To stand in his kayak, Flip has installed a set of Scotty outrigger floats. These floats consist of a sta-bility rod and two plastic bladders that keep the kayak from flipping over. This way, he can paddle to and from his kayak fishing hot spots without the outriggers, then install his stabilizers when he's on the scene. Standing in the kayak is a great advantage when looking for fish on the flats—it can make the difference between catching and just paddling.

There is so much kayak-fishable property along the Gulf Coast that kayak anglers will have no problem finding productive waters. Flip suggests anglers consult the Hook and Line series of fishing maps for more detailed information.

Florida's Gulf Coast
**Anglers: Chrystal Murray and Greg Bowdish,
  Team Ocean Kayak**
Specialty: Snook, reds, sea trout, tarpon

Chrystal and Greg live in kayak fishing heaven. Florida's southwest coast features thousands of square miles of sheltered waters that are chock-full of the world's most prestigious sportfish. "It's an absolutely wonderful place," says Chrystal.

Much of the Gulf Coast—especially the Pine Island/Charlotte Harbor—is covered by a thick growth of mangroves, protecting hidden ponds and bays that motorboaters could never find, let alone access.

Two rods and a packed lunch are all Florida flats fishermen need to find a great day on the water.

But sneaking around in the undergrowth requires some specialized kayak rigging. "Keep it to a minimum," Chrystal says. Greg goes on to explain, "I don't even take a milk crate because it can get in the way." Chrystal still uses the crate to carry her gear from the car to the launch and back. "I can make one trip with rods and tackle, then return to get my boat."

Both anglers use RAM or Scotty rod holders as opposed to flush mounts. "I can lay my rods flat against the kayak to get through the heavy cover," Greg explains. "When you're fishing in clear, shallow water, rods sticking up will actually spook the fish." In addition,

Chrystal points out that these types of rod holders elevate the reels, keeping them out of the corrosive salt water.

Greg touts the advantages of a rudder—"primarily because when you're drifting across the flats, you can use the rudder to control the kayak while the wind pushes you." Almost all of the kayaks he sells at Angler's Outfitters leave the shop with a rudder installed. "If a customer doesn't get a rudder when he buys his boat," Greg goes on, "he usually returns and has one installed."

A stake-out pole is another item both 'yakers recommend. This is a 5-foot-long aluminum or fiberglass pole with a pointed end that is used to secure the kayak in shallow water. Like an anchor, the pole can be speared into the mud or sand then tied to the kayak to keep you in place when stalking fish on the flats. You can also use it in place of the paddle to propel yourself under thick brush and through skinny water. Chrystal also suggests you break down your paddle and use one half like a canoe paddle to pass beneath low-hanging mangroves.

Another key item for flats fishing is a towrope or kayak leash. Most flats anglers use their kayaks as a floating tacklebox—paddling to a fishy area then getting out of the kayak and wading. With a 10-foot piece of rope, you can tether the boat to you while you walk the flats. "You can use the leash to tie off to the mangroves or as a safety item in case you have to tow someone home," Greg goes on. "You can stake off while you're fighting a fish so it doesn't pull you into the bushes. You can get killed being dragged into the trees."

Anglers fishing the Florida flats don't have the luxury of taking a quiver of rods with them into the mangrove jungle. Luckily, one outfit will cover the gamut of skinny-water fish. Since most of the fish are prowling the shallows in mere inches of water, Florida's Gulf Coast anglers can use very light tackle. A 7- to 7½-foot medium-light-action spinning rod and matching reel spooled with 15- to 20-pound braided line will do the trick. Tie a short length of 20- to 30-pound fluorocarbon leader to the braid to hide your intentions from wary fish in clear water. Greg likes to target tarpon from his 'yak, so he takes along a heavier outfit: a 10- to 20-pound-class spinning combo or a 10-weight fly rod.

Florida anglers are also lucky in that they need only a handful of lures to ply the backwaters. Both Chrystal and Greg recommend a selection of jigheads from ⅛ to ¼ ounce and matching soft plastic tails. "You can't go wrong with curly tails in rootbeer and gold," Chrystal says. Greg adds that soft plastic jerkbaits rigged on a weedless hook are popular with the fish. "We're doing weird things; we're more like freshwater bass fishermen," he says.

"You can catch any fish on the flats with a spoon," adds Chrystal. She prefers her flatware in the ⅛- to ¼-ounce size. "You don't need to add trailers or tails—just fish the spoon plain." Greg loves top-water action, especially for tarpon. His favorite popper is the Zoom Honey Toad on conventional tackle—or, when he's using a fly rod, he likes a Rattle Snake fly, which is his own invention. Both anglers stress working these baits slowly. "The spoon should wobble, not spin," Chrystal says while Greg fools tarpon by popping his popper. "*Super* slow."

So, let's see. Minimal rigging, minimal tackle, and miles of skinny water that are accessible only with a paddle, all filled with the sport's most popular gamefish. Yeah—Florida's Gulf Coast sounds like kayak fishing heaven to me.

Florida's East Coast
Angler: Captain Tom Van Horn
Specialty: Reds, trout, snook, tarpon, cobia

Mosquito Lagoon and the Indian River offer Captain Tom Van Horn one of the most diverse fisheries in the continental United States. "The estuary stretches from the temperate north to the tropical south," Van Horn says, "and is home to over 700 species of fish." Between the year-round residents like black drum, red drum, and sea trout, and the seasonal visitors such as snook, tarpon, and cobia, Atlantic coast anglers have a lot to keep them busy.

And there is one way to catch all these species: sight casting. "Ninety percent of the time," Van Horn says, "you've got to see fish to catch them."

Even in the skinniest water, speckled trout cannot hide from a kayaker.

He adds, "We rig boats so you can stand in them." Anglers fishing the flat quiet waters of the Mosquito Lagoon and Indian River are looking for a kayak that has a wide, stable hull and plenty of flat space in the cockpit for their feet. Van Horn has found the perfect craft, a Freedom Hawk 14. This boat looks like a Transformer—from the cartoon series and movie—the stern opens like a Y into a pair of pontoons, allowing you to stand and sight cast to fish.

Van Horn uses a push pole to propel him across the flats and a stake-out pole to stop him in his tracks. "Drift with the wind at your back," he says, "then when you see fish, stick the stake-out pole through the scuppers to stop flat." The Freedom 14 has an anchor release in the bow so Van Horn can simply drop his small grapple anchor when he sees a school of feeding fish.

"Most guys have a RAM tube or Scotty mount in front of them to hold their rod while they pole along," he says, "but I paddle the Freedom facing backward so the rod in the tank well is within reach."

Van Horn recommends anglers take a couple of rods on the water: a light spinning outfit (⅛ to ¾ ounce) for trout and puppy drum and a heavier unit (½ to 2 ounces) for big drum, tarpon, and snook. Each rod should be at least 7½ feet long, sporting a reel spooled with 10- to 20-pound braid to allow for a super-long cast. "We're fishing in inches of water," he says, "and these fish are extremely spooky."

Lure choice depends on the mullet. "In winter when the mullet aren't running, we use shrimp and crab imitations." Rip Tide and Gulp versions of these baits are his favorite. From April through November, when the mullet are in town, Van Horn switches to top-water tackle. "I like a Storm Chug Bug or Rapala Skitter Walk."

Not only are there hundreds of species of fish in the Indian River system, but there are hundreds of places to fish for them. "One unique place is the No Motor Zone, which is a 30-square-mile marine protected area." Because motorboats are not permitted in these waters, the fish get little fishing pressure.

"Paddle until you see fish," Van Horn suggests. "If you don't see fish, keep paddling." He recommends looking for a long sandbar ridge and fishing the shallower water inside for smaller trout and reds, or hunting the deeper water outside for big drum, tarpon, and snook. "The best fishing is 7 miles from the nearest launch," Van Horn says, "but when you get there, you find happy fish."

New England
Angler: Roland St. Denis
Specialty: Striped bass

To fish all year in the Northeast, you have to be an all-weather fisherman. Roland St. Denis and the crew at www.yakdawgs.com have perfected the art of fishing under any conditions. Sure, spring, summer, and fall can be weathered with the standard waders and dry top, but winter requires the big guns. "You've got to have a dry suit," Roland says, "just to be safe." With water temperatures in the low 30s and air temperatures in the teens, 'yak anglers who fish through the winter can't afford even a quick dip in New England water. "We've discovered SealSkinz gloves," he adds. "They're waterproof, warm, and good paddling gloves."

But it isn't only winter weather that gives New England anglers grief; summer, spring, and fall weather can be a challenge, too. You'll be fishing open water with swift current punctuated by huge boulders and shallow sandbars. And often you'll be fishing it at night. "Fog is a big problem," St. Denis notes. "Do not head out without a compass and a GPS." In fact, he carries two GPS units in case one fails when it is needed most.

Another common feature for New England kayaks is flush-mounted rod holders behind the seat. "We do a lot of trolling to find striped bass," Roland explains, "then we break out the lures and cast to the fish." Roland usually starts the day or night pulling tubes and worms. "If you want to tube and worm all day, you'll kill them. You can get into a ton of fish—and it is easy." However, he likes to even the odds on stripers, choosing to bust out the poppers, plugs, or slugs when the fish are thick. When he finds small stripers, he'll scale down to smaller slugs and spoons and jig or cast around structure. "We have a great flats fishery, too," he says, comparing the skinny-water striper fishing to tropical sight casting for bonefish.

Yankee 'yakers' quivers of rods represent the different styles of fishing they do. For trolling Roland picks a medium-heavy to heavy rod—he likes a 7-foot Daiwa Coastal Inshore stick—matched to a conventional reel (such as a Daiwa Luna 300) and spooled with 65-pound-test Spectra line. "The rod is light and it has a short butt, which is perfect for kayak fishing."

Once Roland finds stripers with tube lures, he grabs a 7- to 8-foot medium-action spinning outfit coupled with a Shimano Stradic 4000 series reel loaded with 20- to 30-pound braid. "Some guys go with lighter stuff," he admits, "but we've learned over the years that this only results in lost fish. We like to get the fish to the boat quickly and release them while they're still full of energy."

Of course, huge schools of aggressive striped bass fighting for a limited supply of bait lends itself to throwing flies. Roland chooses a 9-weight rod armed with an intermediate line. "Whether we've got peanuts or big bunker, there's always menhaden around," he says, "so we always keep a variety of bunker patterns on hand." Whether he's using Deceivers, Clousers, or long streamers, he tries to match the size of the fly to the size of whatever the fish are eating. "When the false albacore and bluefin tuna move in," St. Denis adds, "we tie up Bunny Flies and Surf Candies." Very cute.

Roland also stresses the importance of high-quality terminal tackle. "You've got to go with top-of-the-line stuff," he says. "Spend the extra few bucks for the confidence to pull big bass out of the rocks."

When the striper run begins in spring, Roland and his crew target the fish with 9-inch Slug-Gos and Yum Houdini Shad. "We use big rubber when the fish are following herring up the rivers," he says. "At night we pick dark colors like purple or black."

He encourages anglers to be prepared for the blitz. "Always keep a topwater rod rigged with a Gibbs Polaris Popper or Stillwater Popper." There's always a chance of paddling into the middle of school of stripers going berserk on the surface, but the best topwater action is usually early in the morning or just before dark. Roland also favors swimming plugs like a Long A Bomber or Yo-Zuri Crystal Minnow: "You can troll or cast them and late in the season they'll often out produce tubes and worms." When he's night fishing for big bass, he goes with big plugs made by Gibbs and Tattoo's Tackle. Year-round, the Connecticut Kayak Crew finds striper by jigging 1- to 3-ounce Crippled Herring spoons in the deeper channels that run within a couple of miles of the beach.

As for launch locations, "There are a lot of good places around here," Roland says. "Barn Island in Stonington is easy to find, has a good launch, and offers access to many different types of structure." He explains that within a mile of the launch, anglers can fish every type of northern-style structure: rocks, jetties, channels, and sand flats. "It's a mecca for big bass." In Groton, Connecticut, Roland recommends the Bay Berry Lane Launch, which is only a mile from Pine

Island and a short paddle from the mouth of the Thames River. "It's another all-purpose spot," he says. "You can work the rocks around the island, the sand flats east of the launch, or the mouth of the Thames, which is a holdover for winter striper."

It's no wonder kayak anglers love striped bass. Whether you're casting, trolling, jigging, live baiting, or on the fly; whether you're fishing in the channel, along the beach, on the flats, in the rocks, or on the open ocean—you can catch stripers the way you like to fish.

Midwest
Angler: Gary Garth
Specialty: Freshwater fishing for largemouth bass, smallmouth bass, and panfish

For Gary Garth and other sweet-water kayak enthusiasts, paddle power is all about access. "I use my kayak to get into places I would never bring a boat and find fish that have seen very little fishing pressure," he says. To paddle through thick brush and into deep cover, Garth keeps his kayak low-profile. He has installed two Scotty rod holders on either side of his seat. Their cradles are angled parallel to the kayak's gunnels so the rods lie flat along the boat. "I have a bungee cord stretched across the bow that I can slide the rod tips under," he explains. He also packs a single-bladed paddle: "I can scull the kayak with one arm while fishing with the other." This allows him to get into the deepest, darkest freshwater jungles, where the bass have never seen a spinnerbait, plug, or jig.

Since Garth is using his kayak to go where no bassman has gone before, he cannot take along the quiver of fishing rods afforded boat-bound bass anglers. "I only take two rods," he says, "and I try to keep cords, and straps, and other stuff off the boat to keep it as clean as possible." For 'yakers new to bass fishing, he recommends a 6- to 6½-foot light-action spinning outfit for open water and a 5½-foot rod for tight cover. Gary matches these sticks to light reels spooled with 4- to 6-pound test. For the fly division, Garth packs an 8-foot-long 4-weight and a small reel laced with floating line.

Kayak anglers plying the sweet water will have to scale down their rods and cut down their tackle to catch big fish deep in the backwaters.

A handful of tackle is all Garth needs to fool these virgin bass. He recommends attaching a small snap swivel to your line to make lure changes quickly and easily. He likes to pack his tackle into a fishing vest to keep it close at hand. To accommodate the vest, Garth has gone to using an inflatable PFD that stays out of the way until he needs it.

He fills the tackle vest with in-line Mepps spinners in size 1 and 2, adding two or three colors of small Rebel Trackdown minnows, a couple of Pop-R surface plugs, and a handful of medium-sized ⅛- to ¼-ounce spinnerbaits. "My personal preference with the hard baits is to replace the treble hooks with single hooks—it makes them safer to use and easier to release fish." Garth has found this selection to work for almost everything that swims in fresh water. "For smallmouths," he notes, "you can just size down the lures. The Trackdowns in silver and white have been really effective." His fly box is as tight as his conventional arsenal. "I take a couple of poppers in sizes 4 to

6, and Woolly Buggers in the 6 to 10 range. Some streamers colored silver and gold with a fleck of white will imitate shad."

Paddling into freshwater fishing can be intimidating for kayak anglers—there's so much ground to cover and so many places to fish. "Pick a cove with access to deep water that is out of the way of boaters, out of the wind, pleasant, and safe." Garth recommends never leaving home without a GPS and plenty of batteries. "When you're kayak fishing you've got to plan carefully." He suggests that kayak anglers learn one area well, then venture out to other fishing destinations. "A kayak is quiet, peaceful, and it takes you places other boats can't go."

Mid-Atlantic
Angler: "Kayak" Kevin Whitley
Specialty: Big fish, little fish, redfish, bluefish

With the variety of fish available to Mid-Atlantic anglers and the range of fishing conditions these guys face, their kayaks have to be rigged like a Swiss Army knife. From big game to skinny water, a 'yaker fishing the backwater bays and adjoining Atlantic Ocean should be equally at home blasting through the surf and across wind-whipped waves as skimming through the flats and navigating salt marshes.

Local kayak fishing legend "Kayak" Kevin Whitley looks for a boat that can cover it all. "There is no such thing as a beginner kayak," he says. "You will end up fishing in open water, so you want to know the boat can handle rough conditions." For Mid-Atlantic kayak fishing, a 'yak must also be capable of covering distance. "Our rule of thumb is: *If you can see it, you can fish it.*" That is, if he can see a destination 3 to 4 miles away, he knows he can reach it with his kayak. "Anything more than that," he adds, "and you spend more time paddling than fishing, and safety becomes a major issue."

Whitley rigs his kayak to meet any fishing situation imaginable, with vertical rod holders on his crate to carry rods and flush-mounted holders in front of his cockpit and behind his seat to accommodate rods for trolling, anchoring, or drifting. "You've got to be able to place your rods at any angle," he says, "to keep the lines straight no matter what direction the boat is facing."

The kayak should also be outfitted with an anchor trolley to position the boat's bow or stern into the current. Whitley often fishes heavy structure such as rocks and pilings, so he has devised a kayak wreck anchor. It's a beefed-up version of an anchor sinker—the type used by pier fishermen—consisting of a 16-ounce glob of lead with four heavy-gauge wire tines sticking out of it. When the tines are bent up, the anchor sticks into the rocks or grapples around a piling. When Whitley pulls on the rope, the tines bend straight and the anchor comes loose.

Toothy critters, like this chopper blue, should be handled with care.

Kevin's arsenal of rods also reflects the region's diverse fishery—but he admits that an angler new to the area can get away with three weapons. "You'll need a light spinning rod spooled with 8- to 15-pound braid for specks, flounder, and puppy drum in the shallows," he says. For tog, sheepshead, and casting 1- to 2-ounce lures as well as light trolling duties, he tells anglers to look for a medium-heavy conventional outfit spooled with 20- to 30-pound braid. "The medium rod should be light and sensitive." To go toe-to-toe with the big boys—big cobia, bull drum, and cow stripers—he recommends a heavier-action rod suited for 1 to 5 ounces of lead and loaded with 40- to 60-pound braid.

Even if it only takes three rods to tame nearly everything that swims the Mid-Atlantic, it takes a garageful of tackle to fool these fish. Whitley's tackle locker includes everything from ⅛-ounce lead-heads and 3-inch Gulp jigs to 12-ounce Mojo sinkers and 9-inch shad tails. For light work in the shallows he uses jigheads from ⅜ to ⅝ ounce dressed in any style of Gulp swimmer. For striper trolling, he rigs 9-inch Tomic plugs, big swimming shad, bunker spoons, 8- to 12-ounce Mojo sinkers, and deep-diving Rapala plugs. For bait fishing, he relies on Owner cutting-edge hooks using 3/0 to 4/0 variants for tog and sheepshead, 8/0 circles to soak chunks of bait for cobia and big drum, and 9/0 J-hooks to dangle live eels in the face of hungry stripers. Kevin adds a handful of nearly every weight of sinker and size of snap and barrel swivel as well as spools of fluorocarbon leader covering 30- to 80-pound test.

Not only must Mid-Atlantic kayak anglers be prepared to meet any weather condition in the pursuit of all kinds of fish, but they must also be able to do so at night. "Some of our best fishing opportunities are after dark," Kevin says. "I probably spend more time fishing at night than during the day." To make his kayak shine, he uses a battery-powered 360-degree white navigation light, which keeps him visible to both motorboaters and other 'yakers. He relies on a lightweight headlamp for close work. "I really like a lamp with a red light—it keeps my pupils from bugging out."

There are so many places to fish along the Mid-Atlantic coast, and so many fish to target, that Whitley suggests you begin shallow and move deep. "Start out fishing the marshy areas, then move to the bays and inlets before heading to the open water." With limitless fishing opportunities for a wide variety of fish available year-round, Whitley warns Mid-Atlantic kayak anglers: "Be careful—you will become addicted."

Index